Against New Heresies

Against New Heresies

H.H. POPE SHENOUDA III

Translated by
St. Mary and St. Moses Abbey

Against New Heresies
By Pope Shenouda III

Translated from Arabic by St. Mary & St. Moses Abbey.

The Arabic text was taken from His Holiness Pope Shenouda III, *Bi'daa Ha'ditha* [New Heresies]. (Cairo, Egypt: The Theological School in Aba'siya—Cairo, 2006).

Copyright © 2024 Coptic Orthodox Diocese of the Southern U.S.A.

All rights reserved.

Designed & Published by:
St. Mary & St. Moses Abbey Press
101 S Vista Dr., Sandia, TX 78383
stmabbeypress.com

All Scripture quotations in the footnotes of this book, unless otherwise indicated, are taken from the New King James Version® Copyright © 1982 by Thomas Nelson, Inc. Used by permission. All rights reserved.

Contents

Introduction 7

1 Fighting Against Punishment and the Requirements of the Divine Justice 9
2 On Punishment 15
3 The Principle of Judgment and Punishment 23
4 The Curse as a Divine Punishment 31
5 The Meaning of "Free Remission" 39
6 The Meaning of "You Were Bought at a Price" 45
7 Sin is Directed Against God 51
8 How was the Redemption of Humankind Accomplished? 55
9 On the Mystery of the Eucharist 91
10 The Body of Christ and the Mystical Body 117
11 The War Against the Law and Works 135
12 The Deification of Man 161
13 Partakers of the Divine Nature 181
14 On the Union of the Divinity with the Humanity 191
15 Against Biblical Criticism 199
16 Interpretation of the Scriptures is as the Scriptures Themselves 211
17 Other Church Mysteries, Besides the Seven Mysteries 213
18 The Efficacy of the Mystery of Matrimony Spiritually 215
19 Against the Doctrine of Redemption, A Soul in Place of a Soul 217
20 Concerning the Author's Book on the Sins of the Flesh 223
21 On the Incarnation 233
22 On the Equality with the Lord Christ and with the Father 245

Introduction

The danger of these new heresies is that they originate from people[1] who are within the Church—or who were so. Of their danger also is that these heresies are used to express the Orthodox faith.

And what is more serious than all this is that they attribute their [own] error to the saints, either through their misunderstanding of what the saints say, or because of their poor translation of their [the saints'] sayings, or through a tinge of allegation against the saints. And another danger is that they spread their ideas.

And some of these, while explaining their thinking, attack the divine revelation.

Others of them have lived abroad and have become influenced by the ideological deviations that are there. And yet others, though have not been abroad, have read books published by Western writers, have become influenced by them, have adopted them, and have desired to spread what they have adopted.

And some love a new opinion, the foreign, anomalous, and

---

1 Almost throughout this book, H.H. Pope Shenouda III purposefully does not mention by name the inventors of the heresies addressed in this book. Rather, His Holiness refers to them as "the writer" or "the author." The reasoning behind this is that His Holiness preferred to address and correct the erroneous ideas, rather than dealing with specific individuals. Nevertheless, His Holiness mentions specific books by name and includes quotes from indicated pages. In this English translation, we have not included the titles of the mentioned Arabic books nor the page numbers, as they would be of no profit to the English reader. We, nevertheless, have included a translation of the quoted passages. If anyone is interested to know the book titles and page numbers mentioned in Arabic, they may refer to the original Arabic text.

they see in spreading it self-glory—for he now knows what others do not.

Or he may have come to offer his readers a new concept, in which there is a tinge of innovation, and perhaps it may not be innovative, but is the mere transmission of known ideas outside our country, where there may not be anyone responding to them.

Therefore, I see that it is our duty to reveal these foreign ideas and respond to them, so that those spreading them may not become wise in their own eyes[2].

When these, through their errors, feared punishment, they therefore began attacking the principle of punishment in general, even though it originates from God Himself. And the statement "divine justice" became heavy upon their ears, even [to the extent] that they do not accept in the work of redemption that the Lord Christ took away the punishment on our behalf, through His crucifixion, that the divine justice may take its due.

Therefore, I would like to begin by this exact point, for it will lead us to discover many errors of this group of writers.

Pope Shenouda III

---

[2] See Proverbs 26:5.

CHAPTER ONE

Fighting Against Punishment and the Requirements of the Divine Justice

Someone says, "God does not punish anyone, does not kill anyone," and, "Rather, man punishes himself, puts himself to death," and also, "It is true that God gives man the option between life and death. And man, by his will, has chosen death. But man always projects his emotions and suffering, attributing them to God Himself as a horrifying judge."

These statements, however, contain numerous mistakes, though the writer attributes them to Louis Évely. The publisher of these ideas is mistaken, and the one who spreads these ideas is also mistaken by spreading what is erroneous without responding to it.

For God has punished many, from the beginning in the Book of Genesis. He punished Adam, Eve, and the serpent[3], He punished Cain[4], He punished the old world by the flood[5], He punished the people of Sodom by burning the city[6], He also punished the builders of the tower of Babel[7], and He punished with many other punishments in the Book of Genesis and other books.

But the author of the book who says that he is "a Reader[8] in

---

3   See Genesis 3.
4   See Genesis 4.
5   See Genesis 6 and 7.
6   See Genesis 19.
7   See Genesis 11.
8   This is one of the Orders of the Church.

the Coptic Orthodox Church," comments on these punishments appearing in Genesis, saying the following: "The writer of Genesis attributes to God man's punishment and his suffering, as though it were out of God's vengeance for His honor on this creature who has insulted Him. But God forbid."

By using the statement, "the writer of Genesis," and attacking him [i.e. Moses] for attributing to God what He did not do, though He actually did, indicates that the writer [of the previously mentioned book] does not believe that the Book of Genesis is given by inspiration of God. While St. Paul the Apostle says about the Holy Scripture, "All Scripture is given by inspiration of God, and is profitable for doctrine."[9] And St. Peter the Apostle says about the divine Scriptures, "For prophecy never came by the will of man, but holy men of God spoke as they were moved by the Holy Spirit."[10]

So, if the author of the book does not believe that the Book of Genesis is given by inspiration of God, he is neither Christian, nor Jewish, nor even a Reader[11] in the Church. And if he believes that the Book of Genesis is given by inspiration of God, he cannot then say that God has not punished anyone.

For those who perished in the flood did not put themselves to death, but God put them to death.

And those who were burned in Sodom did not burn themselves, but God burned them.

And those whose language was confused in Babel did not themselves confuse their language, but God punished them by this, for their pride.

But if he said that those who drowned in the flood and those burned in Sodom were the cause of their death by their deeds, we would say that their death is a sentence of God who sentenced that "the wages of sin is death."[12] And it is God who said to man in Deuteronomy, "See, I have set before you today life and good,

---

9 2 Timothy 3:16.
10 2 Peter 1:21.
11 A deacon in the Church.
12 Romans 6:23.

death and evil, ... therefore choose life."¹³

For if any man, through his freedom, has chosen death, then he has rather chosen the punishment of God on the sin, which is death. Therefore, how can it be then said that God does not punish anyone, and does not put anyone to death?

The author goes on to say, "The result of sin—that is, returning to nothingness, to the dust with death—was a natural result according to the universal law which God placed, that 'the wages of sin is death.' But God is not the executioner¹⁴ who carries out the sentences, but man is the executioner of himself, and he kills himself by his sin." And this sarcasm in using the word "executioner" is not befitting when speaking of God. For God, undoubtedly, is the one who executes the sentence, although man's sin is the reason. For man is the one causing it, but God is the executioner.

As for the statement that man returns to nothingness, this is what Jehovah's Witnesses believe. So, does the author believe in this Jehovah's Witnesses' belief? As for his saying, "returning to nothingness, to the dust," dust is not nothingness on the one hand, and on the other hand, after this dust there will be resurrection and the life of the coming age—and there is no nothingness in this.

The author goes on to say: "God, who is love and all giving, does not produce evil nor death."

In whose hand then is death? Life and death are in God's hand. He kills and makes alive. "I have the keys of Hades and of death."¹⁵ And He is the one who said in Deuteronomy, "I kill and I make alive."¹⁶ And He is the one who pronounces the sentence of death, as He said, "The soul who sins shall die."¹⁷ So, is it true that God does not punish anyone? When He sent His angel, who struck Herod, and he died because he did not give glory to God,¹⁸ did

---

13 Deuteronomy 30:15, 19.
14 The word used in the text is slang for "executioner."
15 Revelation 1:18.
16 Deuteronomy 32:39.
17 Ezekiel 18:20.
18 See Acts 12:23.

He not punish anyone? And if I say that Herod had caused his own death by his pride, then this would mean that he had exposed himself to God's judgment of death.

Death is God's judgment since Adam, for the Lord said to him, "In the day that you eat of it you shall surely die."[19] God's punishment, then, and chastisement have been from the beginning, since Adam.

The author says: "The story of Original Sin makes it clear that Adam was stripped of grace by merely eating. And this is the spiritual death." And his being stripped of grace, was this not a punishment? That is, the grace of God had left him.

And the author further elaborates—or is further entangled—by rejecting divine punishment, saying, "God is innocent of this injustice which attributes punishment to Him!" This is marvelous! Did not God punish David for his falling into adultery and murder?[20] Did not God punish Moses by not letting him enter the promised land?[21] Did He not punish Saul the king, so that it was said of him that "the Spirit of the LORD departed from Saul, and a distressing spirit from the LORD troubled him"[22]? Did He not punish Korah, Dathan, and Abiram, so that the earth opened its mouth and swallowed them up?[23] Did not the Lord punish the people of Israel for their errors, and deliver them into being carried away to Babylon?[24]

The author also comments on the Old Testament punishments, saying, "For so did the writers of the Old Testament understand justice, as did the disciples understand when they asked God that fire may come down upon those who did not receive Him." The statement "the writers of the Old Testament" means that he does not believe that the Holy Scriptures of the Old Testament are given by inspiration. It is marvelous that these people impose their opinion

---

19   Genesis 2:17.
20   See 2 Samuel 12.
21   See Deuteronomy 3:23–27.
22   1 Samuel 16:14.
23   See Numbers 16:32.
24   See 2 Kings 21:12–14.

on the Holy Scriptures and criticize the Books of Scripture that are not in agreement with them, as though they were man-made.

The author tries to speak about God's love in removing the punishment, so he holds on to what is said in the Divine Liturgy According to St. Gregory: "[You] have turned for me the punishment into salvation." And this statement, while speaking of God's salvation, at the same time confirms that there was punishment. And this punishment, of course, came from God, and it was in need of the work of redemption.

And although the Old Testament sacrifices were symbols of this redemption, the author did not understand these sacrifices in their symbolic meaning, so he says with derision: "What pleasure [is there], I ask you, in seeing slaughtering and the pouring of blood, which are grievous to see, except from a God who is sadistic and cruel, who is not silenced except if He takes vengeance on His enemy?" The sadist is a person who takes delight in violence. And here the author asks: "Is this the heavenly Father? God forbid. This erroneous understanding might be understood from a quick reading of the sacrifices in Leviticus ..." This is marvelous! Does the author not consider it sadistic and cruel for him to eat meat, through pouring out the blood of these animals, while he considers it sadistic and cruel if the blood [of animals] was a symbol of the blood of Christ in His redemption of humankind? I need to explain this to him so that he does not consider God to be a sadist who delights in the pouring of blood.

And what is marvelous is that the author relies on the writings of atheists, by whom he was influenced. And he presents these writings to prove his idea against punishment. For he says that contemporary atheism has called for the freedom of man and his honor, in facing a sadistic God whom Christians portrayed—though unintentionally—as Someone who always desires punishment for His honor; or who coerces a person to love Him by force if he wants life. Therefore, the atheist philosopher, Nietzsche, proclaimed that God is dead, and that man may be set free.

And he reiterates the description of God as a sadist, using as an example "what Mounier called theological sadism, and he had described it as the humiliation of the human condition."

Justice and Chastening

The justice of God demands that He does not equate the innocent with the guilty, and demands that the innocent be recompensed and that the guilty be punished. And it is said of Him in the Second Coming that "He will reward each according to his works,"[25] and it is also said, "For whom the Lord loves He chastens.... For what son is there whom a father does not chasten? But if you are without chastening, ... then you are illegitimate and not sons."[26] And God punished Eli the priest because he did not chasten his sons.[27]

If there were no punishments, people would be led to heedlessness. If God were not characterized by justice, this would be a deficiency in Him—God forbid! And he who lives in righteousness does not fear the justice of God but is pleased by it.

Finally, I have not mentioned the name of the person who published the previous errors and others, to give him an opportunity to repent. And he who has ears to hear, let him hear.

---

25 Matthew 16:27.
26 Hebrews 12:6–8.
27 See 1 Samuel 3.

CHAPTER TWO

On Punishment

Those fighting against the justice of God deny an attribute of His essence as a just Judge and focus only on His mercy and His love. And if they fight against the justice of God in the name of mercy, let them know that the attributes of God are inseparable from each other. For the justice of God is a merciful justice, and the mercy of God is a just mercy.

And in focusing on the love of God, they ignore many verses that speak about His justice, or try to interpret them in such a way that they may go along with their own thinking. And if they sometimes include sayings of the Fathers, they quote them with brevity, as though pulling out a statement without indicating the context it was said in. And in this manner also they do with respect to their quoting from the Divine Liturgy.

For example, they may quote the statement: "[You] have turned for me the punishment into salvation."[28] They focus on the word "salvation," while ignoring that it is salvation from punishment. Nevertheless, they with all boldness say that God does not punish anyone. And when they use the statement: "You have lifted the curse of the Law,"[29] they focus on the Lord Christ's redemptive work in His lifting the curse of the Law from us, forgetting that God is the one who placed these curses upon everyone who breaks His commandments.[30] And when they quote: "You have given

---

28 The Divine Liturgy According to St. Gregory – Agios [Holy].
29 Ibid.
30 See Deuteronomy 27–28.

me the Law as a help," they focus on the expression "as a help," forgetting that the Law was a help concerning guidance, but it was also a scale for justice and judgment, that people may be judged according to the words of that Law.

Time would fail me if I included all the examples of their quoting, but I will say that they, for the sake of focusing on the love of God, deny all the words of punishment. For they deny the punishment of death, the punishment of the curse, and all that pertain to the everlasting torment. And they consider that God has no business nor dispensation in all this!

They say that man is the one causing all this to himself, through his free will. And we do not deny that man is the cause for his falling into punishment, but at the same time, he is the one who has made himself subject to the judgment of God. And death—and perdition—is nothing but a punishment pronounced by God Himself. The curse—and the everlasting torment—is nothing but a punishment pronounced by God Himself. So how can it be said that they are not of God's dispensation[31]?

The Punishment of Death

The first time the word "death" appeared in the Holy Scriptures was from the mouth of God and of God's judgment.

It was He who said to the first man about the forbidden tree that "in the day that you eat of it you shall surely die."[32] So how can a person dare and say: "Even when we say that death is the judgment of God upon the sinner, it does not mean that death is of the dispensation and making of God at all, but the word 'judgment' means 'evaluation' or 'diagnosis'"?

And how does he also say, "God created us for life, and did not create or dispense the judgment of death at all"? It is true that He created us for life, but He pronounced the judgment of death[33]

---

31 Or: economy.
32 Genesis 2:17.
33 Literally: He sentenced with death.

upon the disobedience. And here, near the end of Deuteronomy, God says, "See, I have set before you today life and good, death and evil."[34]

It is God then who set life—eternal life—[as] a reward for doing good. He also set death [as] a recompense for doing evil. And He repeats the same words in the same chapter, saying, "I have set before you life and death, blessing and cursing; therefore choose life, that you and your descendants may live."[35] So how is it said that this is not of the dispensation[36] of God?

And how, in his meditation on what came in the Divine Liturgy about death—"whereby we were bound and sold on account of our sins,"—he says, "We were sold [through our will] on account of our sins. And death binding us is not of God's will as a punishment."

Indeed, as we say in the Divine Liturgy, "I plucked for myself the sentence of death," we however plucked the sentence of death which God pronounced[37] against us when we sinned.

For our sinful will made us subject to the sentence pronounced by God, [as] a punishment for sin.

And not only is this in the Old Testament, but in the New Testament also. For Paul the Apostle says in his Epistle to the Hebrews: "For if we sin willfully after we have received the knowledge of the truth, there no longer remains a sacrifice for sins, but a certain fearful expectation of judgment, and fiery indignation which will devour the adversaries," till he says, "It is a fearful thing to fall into the hands of the living God."[38]

So do we then deny judgment—first of which is death—in our speech on the love of God?

As for "and death, which entered into the world through the envy of the devil,"[39] this does not mean that the devil is the one

---

34   Deuteronomy 30:15.
35   Deuteronomy 30:19.
36   Or: economy.
37   Or: sentenced.
38   Hebrews 10:26–31.
39   The Divine Liturgy According to St. Basil – Prayer of Reconciliation.

who pronounced the judgment of death. Rather, he was the one who deceived man, to disobey God's commandment, that he may fall into the judgment of death which God pronounced. And so, we say to God in the Divine Liturgy concerning man: "And when he fell through the deception of the enemy and the disobedience of Your holy commandment."[40]

Our fall then was by our will, and through the interference of the devil who envied and deceived us to disobey the holy commandment of God. So we fell into God's sentence[41] to death.

God is the one who pronounces the judgment of death and is the one who lifts it through our repentance.

Therefore, when David repented and regretted his sin, he heard the divine judgment through the mouth of Nathan the prophet: "The LORD also has put away your sin; you shall not die."[42] And in the same chapter, God, the just Judge, imposed punishments on David, and sentenced[43] to death his son who was born of sin, saying, "Because by this deed you have given great occasion to the enemies of the LORD to blaspheme, the child also who is born to you shall surely die."[44]

Nevertheless, the attacker of the justice of God says: "God did not create death."

When God takes away the gift of life from a person, He sentences[45] him to death. And as He said about Himself in Revelation: "And I have the keys of Hades and of Death."[46] And it is He who "kills and makes alive,"[47] and is He who pronounced His judgment, saying, "The soul who sins shall die,"[48] and is He who said about the repentance of the sinner: "But if a wicked man turns

---

40 The Divine Liturgy According to St. Gregory – Prayer of Reconciliation.
41 Or: judgment.
42 2 Samuel 12:13.
43 Or: judged.
44 2 Samuel 12:14.
45 Or: judged.
46 Revelation 1:18.
47 1 Samuel 2:6.
48 Ezekiel 18:4.

from all his sins which he has committed, keeps all My statutes, and does what is lawful and right, he shall surely live; he shall not die."[49]

Do you not see then that [both] life and death are in the hands of God.

This does not prevent for a person, if he walks in the way of righteousness, to be deserving of eternal life which God grants him; and if he walks in the way of sin, he is deserving of death through the judgment of God.

And so many are the judgments of death which God pronounced, among which are:

The judgment of the flood, in which the Lord said, "I will destroy man whom I have created from the face of the earth.... The end of all flesh has come before Me.... And behold, I Myself am bringing floodwaters on the earth, to destroy from under heaven all flesh in which is the breath of life; everything that is on the earth shall die."[50] Yes, this is the flood which that author disparages, who, for the sake of defending the love of God, disrespects the Holy Scriptures.

The judgment which God pronounced on Korah, Dathan, and Abiram, where "the ground split apart under them, and the earth opened its mouth and swallowed them up, with their households.... So they and all those with them went down alive into the pit; the earth closed over them, and they perished from among the assembly."[51] Is this not a divine judgment of death, which Korah and his companions plucked for themselves? It is nevertheless a judgment from God which was carried out in a divine, miraculous way.

The judgment which Peter the Apostle pronounced on Ananias and Sapphira: Peter pronounced it through the authority given to him from God, for he cannot do that through his mere human power. And truly they deserved this, because they lied to

---

49   Ezekiel 18:21.
50   Genesis 6:6, 13, 17.
51   Numbers 16:31–33.

the Holy Spirit.[52] But it is a divine judgment of death.

The Lord likewise sentenced the murderer to death. On this the Lord said after Noah's Ark was anchored: "Surely for your lifeblood I will demand a reckoning.... From the hand of every man's brother I will require the life of man. Whoever sheds man's blood, by man his blood shall be shed; for in the image of God He made man."[53] And so did God demand Abel's blood from the hand of his brother Cain. And He said to him: "Where is Abel your brother?... The voice of your brother's blood cries out to Me from the ground."[54]

The one fighting against divine justice, however, defends the offender, and not the victim, and says: "Destroying the offender is like [destroying] the victim, to satisfy the hatred of the victim, the hatred and thirst for the shedding of blood."

Is it not of justice to protect the weak from the tyranny of strong, by punishing that offender? Otherwise, the law of the wild would prevail, and he who can devour another would have no deterrent from devouring him. God as Pantocrator "executes justice for the oppressed."[55] And it is He who said in the Book of Ezekiel the prophet: "I will feed My flock, and I will make them lie down.... [I] will bind up the broken and strengthen what was sick; but I will destroy the fat and the strong, and feed them in judgment."[56]

The Lord also punished David for killing Uriah the Hittite. He said to him when his punishment was pronounced: "You have killed Uriah the Hittite with the sword; you have taken his wife to be your wife, and have killed him with the sword of the people of Ammon. Now therefore, the sword shall never depart from your house, because you have despised Me."[57]

---

52 See Acts 5:3–4.
53 Genesis 9:5–6.
54 Genesis 4:9–10.
55 Psalms 146:7.
56 Ezekiel 34:15–16.
57 2 Samuel 12:9–10.

And God the Lord has said through the tongue of Paul the Apostle: "Beloved, do not avenge yourselves ... for it is written, 'Vengeance is Mine, I will repay,' says the Lord."[58]

The Lord prohibited David the prophet and king from building the temple, as a punishment for him because of the shedding of blood. And regarding this David said to his son Solomon:

> It was in my mind to build a house to the name of the LORD my God; but the word of the LORD came to me, saying, You have shed much blood and have made great wars; you shall not build a house for My name, because you have shed much blood on the earth in My sight.[59]

Lack of punishment leads to heedlessness. And there are those who are saved with fear. As the Apostle said, "But others save with fear, pulling them out of the fire."[60] As it is also said, "Conduct yourselves throughout the time of your stay here in fear;"[61] and, "Work out your own salvation with fear and trembling."[62] Not all are led with love. For some fear is suitable.

At least in punishing the offender, we are delivering the world from him, and the rest are made to desist. As St. Paul the Apostle said to his disciple Timothy the bishop: "Those who are sinning rebuke in the presence of all, that the rest also may fear."[63]

And what is more is that those fighting against divine justice deny every punishment pronounced by God, saying that He has not cursed any of His creatures, that "He has not cursed the earth as might be thought by those reading the words 'Cursed is the ground for your sake' (Genesis 3:17)," and that He does not recompense nor condemn.

And what is marvelous is that they stand before clear verses,

---

58 Romans 12:19.
59 1 Chronicles 22:7–8.
60 Jude 23.
61 1 Peter 1:17.
62 Philippians 2:12.
63 1 Timothy 5:20.

[yet] they change their interpretation. Therefore, we will continue this response in the following chapters.

CHAPTER THREE

The Principle of Judgment and Punishment

Judgment

The principle of punishment and recompense is clear in the Holy Scriptures and the rites of the Church.

For the Scripture says, "For we must all appear before the judgment seat of Christ, that each one may receive the things done in the body, according to what he has done, whether good or bad."[64] And the Lord Himself explained what will happen in the judgment when they stand before Him in His Second Coming, so He will separate them one from another and judge them, saying to some, "Come, you blessed of My Father, inherit the kingdom prepared for you from the foundation of the world,"[65] and to others, "Depart from Me, you cursed, into the everlasting fire prepared for the devil and his angels."[66] He also said, "For the Son of Man will come in the glory of His Father with His angels, and then He will reward each according to his works."[67] The same words He also said in the Book of Revelation (22:11). St. John of the Revelation said:

And I saw the dead, small and great, standing before God,

---

64 2 Corinthians 5:10.
65 Matthew 25:34.
66 Matthew 25:41.
67 Matthew 16:27.

and books were opened. And another book was opened, which is the Book of Life. And the dead were judged according to their works.... And they were judged, each one according to his works.... And anyone not found written in the Book of Life was cast into the lake of fire.[68]

And in the Orthodox Creed we proclaim our belief in this judgment, where we say of the Lord Jesus, "He is coming again in His glory to judge the living and the dead." And in the litanies of the Twelfth Hour [in the Agpeya], we say, "Behold, I am about to stand before the just judge terrified and trembling because of my many sins. For a life spent in pleasures deserves condemnation." Likewise in the Divine Liturgy According to St. Basil, we say, "He has appointed a Day for recompense, on which He will appear to judge the world in righteousness, and give each one according to his deeds." All these are clear texts about judgement, and there are many others [like them]. So, how does that author say that God does not judge anyone, nor punish anyone?

The condemnation of Satan and all his army of demons

The Scriptures say in the Book of Revelation, "The devil, who deceived them, was cast into the lake of fire and brimstone where the beast and the false prophet are. And they will be tormented day and night forever and ever."[69] Also the Scriptures say, "For if God did not spare the angels who sinned, but cast them down to hell and delivered them into chains of darkness, to be reserved for judgment;"[70] And the Lord Himself says to the devil in the Book of Ezekiel the prophet:

> Therefore I cast you as a profane thing out of the mountain of God; and I destroyed you, O covering cherub, from the midst of the fiery stones. Your heart was lifted up because of your beauty; you corrupted your wisdom for the sake of

---

68 Revelation 20:12–15.
69 Revelation 20:10.
70 2 Peter 2:4.

your splendor; I cast you to the ground.... And I turned you to ashes upon the earth in the sight of all who saw you.[71]

And He says to him [the devil] in the Book of Isaiah the prophet:

For you have said in your heart: "I will ascend into heaven, I will exalt my throne above the stars of God ... I will ascend above the heights of the clouds, I will be like the Most High." Yet you shall be brought down to Sheol, to the lowest depths of the Pit.[72]

Are not all these examples of condemnation[73]? But the devil, from the aforementioned, has received two condemnations: the first condemnation or the first punishment was his being cast to the ground, and the second, which awaits him, is his being cast into the lake of fire and brimstone.

Let us move to another point, that is, the punishments against men.

Punishments

We have spoken about the punishment of death which God pronounced on the sinner, by saying, "The soul who sins shall die."[74] There are many punishments the Holy Scriptures have recorded. Some were pronounced by the Lord Himself, and others through the mouths of His holy apostles, of which we mention the following.

The punishment of the Lord on the cities which rejected Him and did not believe, despite what they saw of His many miracles, by His saying, "Woe to you, Chorazin! Woe to you, Bethsaida! For if the mighty works which were done in you had

---

71   Ezekiel 28:16–18.
72   Isaiah 14:13–15.
73   Or: judgment.
74   Ezekiel 18:4.

been done in Tyre and Sidon, they would have repented long ago in sackcloth and ashes. But I say to you, it will be more tolerable for Tyre and Sidon in the day of judgment than for you. And you, Capernaum, who are exalted to heaven, will be brought down to Hades.... But I say to you that it shall be more tolerable for the land of Sodom in the day of judgment than for you."[75] Note that the repetition of "it shall be more tolerable" indicates the disparity in the degrees [of severity] of punishment in the day of judgment.

The punishment of the Lord on Jerusalem and His judgment of the destruction of the temple, by His saying: "O Jerusalem, Jerusalem, the one who kills the prophets and stones those who are sent to her! How often I wanted to gather your children together, as a hen gathers her chicks under her wings, but you were not willing! See! Your house is left to you desolate."[76]

The punishment which He imposed on sinners who had no spiritual fruit, as He said, "Every branch in Me that does not bear fruit He takes away.... If anyone does not abide in Me, he is cast out as a branch and is withered; and they gather them and throw them into the fire, and they are burned."[77] And as He said in the Sermon on the Mount, "Every tree that does not bear good fruit is cut down and thrown into the fire."[78] Similarly, St. John the Baptist said, "And even now the ax is laid to the root of the trees. Therefore every tree which does not bear good fruit is cut down and thrown into the fire."[79]

Also the sentence of the Lord on the unrepentant to perdition, as He said, "Do you suppose that these Galileans were worse sinners than all other Galileans, because they suffered such things? I tell you, no; but unless you repent you will all likewise perish. Or those eighteen on whom the tower in Siloam fell and killed them, do you think that they were worse sinners than all other men who dwelt in Jerusalem? I tell you, no; but unless you

---

75 Matthew 11:20–24.
76 Matthew 23:37–38.
77 John 15:2, 6.
78 Matthew 7:19.
79 Matthew 3:10.

repent you will all likewise perish."[80] And the Lord repeated twice this statement "unless you repent you will all likewise perish."

The punishment which He placed upon Jezebel in the Book of Revelation, who says that she is a prophetess, that she may teach and seduce the people. He said, "I gave her time to repent … and she did not repent."[81] So He imposed a punishment on her and on those who sin because of her, "unless they repent of their deeds."[82] And the Lord concluded, by saying, "And I will give to each one of you according to your works."[83]

Another example is the "woes" which He poured on the scribes and Pharisees, as it came in Matthew 23, where He revealed to them their mistakes and hypocrisy. He said to them at the end of the "woes," "Serpents, brood of vipers! How can you escape the condemnation of hell?"[84] He also said to them, "That on you may come all the righteous blood shed on the earth, from the blood of righteous Abel to the blood of Zechariah, son of Berechiah, whom you murdered between the temple and the altar."[85] Is not the justice of God made manifest in all these, and are not His punishments made manifest?

Another example of the punishment of God is what the Lord said in the Sermon on the Mount, "Whoever is angry with his brother without a cause shall be in danger of the judgment. And whoever says to his brother, 'Raca!' shall be in danger of the council. But whoever says, 'You fool!' shall be in danger of hell fire."[86] Although these punishments are for the sins of the tongue, the Lord adds also, "For by your words you will be justified, and by your words you will be condemned."[87] Therefore, there is judgment and punishment, not only for sins committed by deed, but also for

---

80 Luke 13:2–5.
81 Revelation 2:21.
82 Revelation 2:22.
83 Revelation 2:23.
84 Matthew 23:33.
85 Matthew 23:35.
86 Matthew 5:22.
87 Matthew 12:37.

the sins of the tongue, and even for looking at a woman to lust for her.[88]

The Lord also mentioned punishments in His parables. He said in the parable of the wheat and the tares:

> Therefore as the tares are gathered and burned in the fire, so it will be at the end of this age. The Son of Man will send out His angels, and they will gather out of His kingdom all things that offend, and those who practice lawlessness, and will cast them into the furnace of fire. There will be wailing and gnashing of teeth.... He who has ears to hear, let him hear![89]

The Lord repeated the same punishment in the parable of the good and bad fish.[90] And in the parable of the ten virgins, the foolish were punished, by the door being shut in their faces, and the Lord said to them, "Assuredly, I say to you, I do not know you."[91] And in the parable of the talents, concerning the servant who had one talent, who hid it in the ground and did not trade with it and make profit, the Lord said, "Cast the unprofitable servant into the outer darkness. There will be weeping and gnashing of teeth."[92] And He repeated the same punishment to the one who came to the wedding without having on a wedding garment.[93] Time would fail us if we spoke about punishment [which appeared] in other parables and sayings.

Punishments pronounced by the Lord's Apostles through an authority from Him: Of these is His saying, "Whatever you bind on earth will be bound in heaven,"[94] and His saying, "If you retain the sins of any, they are retained."[95] All these are punishments.

---

88 See Matthew 5:28–29.
89 Matthew 13:40–43.
90 See Matthew 13:49.
91 Matthew 25:11.
92 Matthew 25:30.
93 See Matthew 22:11–13.
94 Matthew 18:18.
95 John 20:23.

Of the severe punishments is the judgment of death pronounced by St. Peter the Apostle on Ananias and Sapphira, so they died because they lied to the Holy Spirit.[96] Of them also is the severe punishment which St. Paul the Apostle imposed on the Corinthian sinner[97], and his saying to the believers in Corinth, "Put away from yourselves the evil person."[98] This [truly] was a punishment although it was for the sake of the good [of the person], resulting in the repentance of the sinner. The Apostle then asked them to offer him love, "lest perhaps such a one be swallowed up with too much sorrow."[99] This was a punishment; nevertheless, a punishment may be a treatment. This we say to the one denying punishments. Also of the famous punishments is the judgment of Paul the Apostle on Bar-Jesus (Elymas the sorcerer) with blindness, so "he went around seeking someone to lead him by the hand."[100]

It is worthwhile to note that the Lord pronounced earthly punishments, apart from the eternal punishment. For example, He punished Moses the prophet by not permitting him to enter into the land of promise,[101] punished David the prophet with earthly punishments also,[102] and punished the children of Israel who went out of Egypt with death in the Wilderness of Sinai.

---

96 See Acts 5:1–10.
97 See 1 Corinthians 5:5.
98 1 Corinthians 5:13.
99 2 Corinthians 2:7.
100 Acts 13:11.
101 See Deuteronomy 32:52.
102 See 1 Samuel 12.

CHAPTER FOUR

The Curse as a Divine Punishment

I am amazed at a Reader, who is a Christian, who reads the Holy Scriptures and says: "God has not cursed anyone! The curse was never a lawful punishment! The curse is made by the freedom of man, and not of God!"

The first curses mentioned in the Holy Scriptures were a punishment by God and a judgment pronounced from the mouth of God. For as a result of the first sin, God judged the serpent and the ground with a curse. He said to the serpent, "You are cursed.... On your belly you shall go, and you shall eat dust all the days of your life."[103] And He said to Adam, "Cursed is the ground for your sake.... Both thorns and thistles it shall bring forth for you."[104] And when Cain killed his brother, we started to see the curse afflicting man himself. For God said to Cain, "You are cursed from the earth, which has opened its mouth to receive your brother's blood from your hand."[105] And so we see that the curse included three categories of the creation: the serpent, the ground, and man. And it was a curse pronounced from the mouth of God.

Then came the flood, which was a curse that was an all-inclusive destruction. On this the Lord said, "I will destroy man whom I have created from the face of the earth, both man and beast, creeping thing and birds of the air."[106] And the proof that the

---

103 Genesis 3:14.
104 Genesis 3:17–18.
105 Genesis 4:11.
106 Genesis 6:7.

flood was a curse sentenced[107] by God, is that when the ark landed on dry land and Noah offered burnt offerings which God smelled as a soothing aroma, then the Lord said, "I will never again curse the ground for man's sake."[108]

In spite of these obvious biblical texts, the [writer who calls himself] Reader does not accept the words of divine revelation as they appear in the Holy Scriptures, but he says: "God has not cursed the ground, as someone might think, reading 'Cursed is the ground for your sake.'[109] Rather, the curse and blessing are an inseparable part of a very important subject in the Old Testament, and even the entire Bible. And this is 'the everlasting covenant' between God, man, and the creation,[110] which we call 'the law of the universe,' that is the natural law."

We see this as an evasion of the biblical text. For if the curse referred to an everlasting covenant between God, man and the creation, then God would be the one who put in place this covenant. And if the source of the punishment of the curse were the law of the universe, then God would be the one who put in place this law. For He is the Creator of the universe and its Governor. He is the Creator of nature and is the one who put in place the natural law. And there is no other power, as the Communists think. Therefore, the matter, first and last, refers to God, the Source of all the judgments, who said, "Behold, I set before you today a blessing and a curse: the blessing, if you obey the commandments of the LORD ... and the curse, if you do not obey the commandments of the LORD."[111] The Lord repeated these same words in the Book of Deuteronomy again, saying, "I call heaven and earth as witnesses today against you, that I have set before you life and death, blessing and cursing,"[112] and the Lord also said, "You shall put the blessing on Mount Gerizim and the curse on Mount Ebal."[113]

---

107 Or: judged.
108 Genesis 8:21.
109 Genesis 3:17–18.
110 See Isaiah 24:5.
111 Deuteronomy 11:26–28.
112 Deuteronomy 30:19.
113 Deuteronomy 11:29.

The curses of the Law, which the Lord commanded, with which He made a covenant

These curses the Lord commanded the Levites to say on Mount Ebal, and the people shall answer and say, "Amen."[114]

> Cursed is the one who makes a carved or molded image.... Cursed is the one who treats his father or his mother with contempt.... Cursed is the one who moves his neighbor's landmark.... Cursed is the one who makes the blind to wander off the road.... Cursed is the one who perverts the justice due the stranger, the fatherless, and widow.... Cursed is the one who attacks his neighbor secretly.... Cursed is the one who does not confirm all the words of this law by observing them.[115]

Many other curses came against the sins of adultery and uncleanness[116], and yet many others in Deuteronomy 28. This latter chapter includes various kinds of blessings for the one who listens to the voice of the Lord his God, and exceedingly many kinds of curses for the one who does not listen to the voice of the Lord his God. These curses came in 53 verses (Deuteronomy 28:15–68), and the following was said at their end: "These are the words of the covenant which the LORD commanded Moses to make with the children of Israel in the land of Moab, besides the covenant which He made with them in Horeb."[117]

Other curses which the Lord pronounced on particular occasions

For example, He said to our father Abraham, "I will bless those who bless you, and I will curse him who curses you."[118] Here God curses those who curse Abraham. Likewise, He said to the children

---

114 See Deuteronomy 27:13–14.
115 Deuteronomy 27:15–26.
116 Deuteronomy 27:20–23.
117 Deuteronomy 29:1.
118 Genesis 12:3.

of Israel, "That you may cut yourselves off and be a curse and a reproach among all the nations of the earth."[119] He also said, "'For I have sworn by Myself,' says the LORD, 'that Bozrah shall become a desolation, a reproach, a waste, and a curse. And all its cities shall be perpetual wastes.'"[120] The Lord also said, "Cursed is he who does the work of the LORD deceitfully,"[121] and, "For he who is hanged [that is crucified] is accursed of God."[122] He also said about the sinful Jerusalem, "Moreover I will make you a waste and a reproach among the nations that are all around you.... So it shall be a reproach, a taunt[123], a lesson..."[124] And it was said in the Book of Zechariah, "This is the curse that goes out over the face of the whole earth."[125] All these are judgments from God.

Curses pronounced by men of God, through an authority He gave them

For example, the curse of our father Noah to Canaan, by his saying, "Cursed be Canaan; a servant of servants he shall be to his brethren."[126] And this curse remained prevalent. Our Lord Jesus Christ relied on this in His speech with the Canaanite woman.[127] Another example is the curse of Elisha the prophet on some youths in the name of the Lord, which was fulfilled in them.[128] Also our father Isaac, in blessing his son Jacob, said to him, "Cursed be everyone who curses you."[129]

Curses pronounced by the Lord Christ

---

119 Jeremiah 44:7.
120 Jeremiah 49:13.
121 Jeremiah 48:10.
122 Deuteronomy 21:23.
123 "A curse" in Arabic text.
124 Ezekiel 5:14–15.
125 Zechariah 5:3.
126 Genesis 9:25. Also see Genesis 9:26–27.
127 See Matthew 15:22, 26.
128 See 2 Kings 2:23–24.
129 Genesis 27:29.

The Lord Christ also cursed the fig tree and those on His left. Concerning the fig tree, He said, "Let no one eat fruit from you ever again."[130] And Peter said to Him, "Rabbi, look! The fig tree which You cursed has withered away."[131] And the Lord also said to the wicked men who were on His left, "Depart from Me, you cursed, into the everlasting fire prepared for the devil and his angels."[132] And the Lord mentions the reason for this as a punishment for them, in His saying, "For I was hungry and you gave Me no food; I was thirsty and you gave Me no drink; I was a stranger and you did not take Me in…. Assuredly, I say to you, inasmuch as you did not do it to one of the least of these, you did not do it to Me."[133]

Therefore, how does someone say, "The curse was never a lawful punishment"?

Were not the curses proclaimed on Mount Ebal a punishment on the one who treats his father or his mother with contempt? Or on the one who makes the blind to wander off the road, or the one who commits adultery or lies with those forbidden? Or on he who kills, the one who makes a carved or molded image, etc.?[134] Or, were not the curses that came in Deuteronomy 28 a punishment, where the following is said in the beginning, "If you do not obey the voice of the LORD your God, to observe carefully all His commandments … that all these curses will come upon you and overtake you."[135]

As for the statement [which the writer who calls himself Reader makes,] that "the curse is made by the freedom of man, and not God," we respond to this by saying that there is a difference between "making" [the curse] and "worthiness" [of the curse], or "sentence" [with a curse] and "worthiness." God is the one who pronounced the sentence with the curse, and man deserved this divine judgment through deviating by his human will toward evil. And he did not make the curse for himself.

---

130 Mark 11:14.
131 Mark 11:21.
132 Matthew 25:41
133 Matthew 25:42–45.
134 See Deuteronomy 27:15–25.
135 Deuteronomy 28:15.

Likewise, it was God who pronounced the sentence[136] with death on the sinner, by His saying, "The soul who sins shall die."[137] And man deserved God's sentence with his death, and he is not the maker of the sentence himself, to himself, and in himself. It is true that the curse is the fruit of man's sin, with which he was deserving of God's sentence on him with the curse. And although it may be a part of the law of the universe, the one who put in place this law of the universe is God.

God's removal of the curse

As for God's removal of the curse, it depends on man's repentance and his benefiting from redemption. And this is clear from the Lord's saying, "Unless you repent you will all likewise perish."[138] And it is also clear from St. Peter's saying to the Jews on Pentecost, "Repent, and let every one of you be baptized in the name of Jesus Christ for the remission of sins,"[139] and from his saying also regarding the acceptance of the Gentiles, of what the hearers repeated that "God has also granted to the Gentiles repentance to life."[140]

Then God does not remove the curse without repentance, but through faith, Baptism, and repentance, man receives salvation, and consequently, the removal of the curse through the worthiness of the blood [of Christ] shed on his behalf.[141]

The phrase that the curse is deprivation of grace

This also is up to God, for He is the one who grants grace, and is the one who deprives some of His grace. Therefore, if He deprived him of His grace and he fell into the curse, this would be a judgment from God, and man is deserving of it. As the Spirit of God came upon Saul

---

136 Or: judgment.
137 Ezekiel 18:4 and 18:20.
138 Luke 13:3 and 13:5.
139 Acts 2:38.
140 Acts 11:18.
141 See Mark 16:16; Acts 2:38; Luke 13:3 and 13:5.

the king, and he prophesied[142], then the Spirit of God departed from him, and a distressing spirit from the Lord troubled him[143].

We should not say then that man, through his sin, can make blessing and grace cease from the earth. Rather, the sound expression is that God makes blessing and grace cease from the earth, because of man's sin. The one who grants the blessing is the one who withholds it. He alone has authority in both cases, and man has no authority to grant or withhold. Man is the cause, but the authority is God's.

As for the saying of that [writer who calls himself] Reader that "God does not take away the blessing by His will from man, not even from evil men," this statement is neither theologically sound[144] nor biblical. Is not God the Giver of the law concerning blessing and cursing?[145] Is not God the one who, by His will, commanded the cherubim to guard the way to the tree of life with a flaming sword, lest Adam eat of it while he is in a state of sin?[146] But in the Book of Revelation: "To him who overcomes I will give to eat from the tree of life."[147]

"He who has an ear, let him hear."[148]

All the curses of the law, Christ bore on our behalf

And so the Apostle said, "Christ has redeemed us from the curse of the law, having become a curse for us (for it is written, 'Cursed is everyone who hangs on a tree')."[149]

And here someone becomes zealous and says, "How can it be said that the Father poured a curse and wrath upon His Son, that He may punish Him instead of us on the cross (Martin Luther), that He may take revenge for the right of His justice and law?! ... For was the

---

142 See 1 Samuel 10:9–10.
143 See 1 Samuel 16:14.
144 "Theologically sound" is literally "theological."
145 See Deuteronomy 11:30.
146 See Genesis 3:22–24.
147 Revelation 2:7.
148 Ibid.
149 Galatians 3:13.

death of the Lord sanctification for humanity and planting of life, or was it a curse?" As a proof of that he says, "The Old Testament sacrifices were not a source of a curse nor did they bear a curse, but were most holy. And man cannot offer a cursed sacrifice to God."

And the answer is that Christ was not cursed—God forbid—but was a bearer of a curse; and He was not crucified while a sinner, but a bearer of sins. And because of His love for us, in bearing our sins and our curse, He was glorified through His crucifixion.

And so, He, having determined to offer Himself on our behalf, said to the Father, "Glorify Your Son, that Your Son also may glorify You,"[150] that is, glorify Him in His love for men, so that He may bear their suffering, sins, and the curses that had fallen upon them, and He may save them. "Greater love has no one than this, than to lay down one's life for his friends."[151]

The sacrifices were in the same state. They were without sin, bearing the sins of someone else. And because they died on behalf of someone else, they were considered most holy. The sacrifice was not cursed, but bore the curse which the one offering it deserves. The burnt offering endured remaining in the fire, wherein it was burned, till it turned into ashes, whereupon the ashes were carried to a clean place.[152] For they were a symbol of giving oneself with respect to man, and a symbol of obedience and submission to God, and so they were considered most holy.

As for the Father, He was not punishing the Son, but was pleased with His suffering, in that by His crucifixion He became a Savior of men. And for[153] this salvation, He sent Him to be the propitiation on our behalf.[154] The Son was not the object of the anger of God, but He bore the anger of God [which was] on sinners. And the Son too despised the shame and endured the cross, for the joy that was set before Him.[155]

---

150 John 17:1.
151 John 15:13.
152 See Leviticus 6:11.
153 Literally: by.
154 See 1 John 4:10.
155 See Hebrews 12:2.

CHAPTER FIVE

The Meaning of "Free Remission"

There is no free remission. For the price of remission is the blood of Christ. Therefore, the Scripture says, "Without shedding of blood there is no remission."[156] Therefore, the sinner in the Old Testament used to offer sacrifices to receive remission. All [the sacrifices] were a symbol of the blood of Christ. And whoever reads about the day of atonement in Leviticus, obtains an idea regarding the sacrifices which atone for sins.[157]

Then, the statement "free remission" is against the doctrine of Incarnation and redemption. For if remission were free [of charge], why did God then send His only begotten Son into the world "to be the propitiation for our sins"[158]? Why was it said, "For God so loved the world that He gave His only begotten Son, that whoever believes in Him should not perish but have everlasting life"[159]? And why was it said, "For indeed Christ, our Passover, was sacrificed for us"[160]? We have not received remission freely, but we "were bought at a price"[161] "with the precious blood of Christ, as of a lamb without blemish and without spot."[162]

What is the meaning then of the statement, "being justified

---

156 Hebrews 9:22.
157 See Leviticus 16.
158 1 John 4:10.
159 John 3:16.
160 1 Corinthians 5:7.
161 1 Corinthians 6:20.
162 1 Peter 1:19.

freely by His grace through the redemption that is in Christ Jesus, whom God set forth as a propitiation by His blood, through faith"[163]? It means that there is a price, that is, the redemption. We did not, however, pay this price, but Christ paid it by His blood. And we received this justification freely, without paying a price, through faith in His blood.

And although Christ paid for [our] remission by His blood instead of us, we will not receive [this remission] except with conditions. There is a difference between the price of remission and the conditions for becoming worthy of [receiving] remission. There are at least three conditions: Faith, repentance, and Baptism.

As for faith, it is made clear from the saying of the Scripture, "...that whoever believes in Him should not perish but have everlasting life."[164] "But he who does not believe is condemned already, because he has not believed in the name of the only begotten Son of God."[165] And it was also said, "He who believes in the Son has everlasting life; and he who does not believe the Son shall not see life, but the wrath of God abides on him."[166] There is then no free remission for those who do not believe, but the wrath of God abides on them.

As for repentance [and Baptism], it is clear from the saying of the Lord, "Unless you repent you will all likewise perish."[167] The Scripture also says, "Then God has also granted to the Gentiles repentance to life."[168] On Pentecost also, when the Jews asked our fathers the Apostles, "'Men and brethren, what shall we do?' Then Peter said to them, 'Repent, and let every one of you be baptized in the name of Jesus Christ for the remission of sins.'"[169] There is then no free remission, without repentance and Baptism. And the Lord

---

163 Romans 3:24–25.
164 John 3:16.
165 John 3:18.
166 John 3:36.
167 Luke 13:3 and 13:5.
168 Acts 11:18.
169 Acts 2:37–38.

likewise said, "He who believes and is baptized will be saved."[170]

Therefore, does anyone dare to say that there is free remission without faith, repentance, or Baptism? The word "freely" means "with nothing in return." But there is a price and conditions. The price Christ paid, and the conditions are obligatory for us and are necessary to receive remission. For despite the great redemption which the Lord Christ offered and despite His precious blood which was shed, there is no possibility for salvation of the unbelievers and unrepentant.

The one speaking of free remission presents objections or remarks, with which he attacks divine justice on remission, and so he mentions the following.

The sinful woman caught in the very act[171]

He says: "They brought her to the just Lord Christ and challenged His justice… The justice of the Law of Moses which judges the crime of the adulteress… so did the Christ act justly?! Was there in His saying, 'He who is without sin among you, let him throw a stone at her first…. Neither do I condemn you; go [in peace] and sin no more'—was there justice in this saying? According to human justice, Christ was not just. According to divine love, this is the justice and the life."

We say that the Lord Christ, in delivering the adulteress from being stoned, was just and was loving, and His love can never be separated from His justice. So how is that? How do we prove His justice in delivering her from being stoned?

1. She was caught in the very act. That is, there were two sinners committing adultery: a man and a woman. So they took the woman, to stone her, but left the man [free] and did not present him to receive a punishment for his committing adultery. Justice is the punishment of the two, for there is no woman committing adultery without there being a man participating in sin with her. So

---

170 Mark 16:16.
171 John 8:3–11.

why would the woman be punished alone?

This matter reminds me of a poem I read in early forties in the Journal of Social Affairs, more than fifty years ago, about a sinful woman, of whom the poet says:

Did you ask those renouncing you as evil,
         How many lecherous are among them concealed?

Fasting, they break their fast on blood;
         Thirsty, drinking blood to inebriation.

They called you a passionate seller of iniquity.
         They lied for the sin is that of the buyer.

Justice then is that the woman should not be stoned alone.

2. Those presenting her to be stoned are themselves sinners too. So why was she to be punished, while they remain unpunished? Therefore, justice was to deliver her [from death]. And so did the Lord say to them, "He who is without sin among you, let him throw a stone at her first."[172] For if justice ordained that sinners were to be punished, then all ought to be treated without discrimination. Christ then was just when He said, "He who is without sin among you, let him throw a stone at her first."

3. As for His saying "Neither do I condemn you,"[173] it means, "Neither do I condemn you alone," for at the same time He did condemn her sin, by saying to her, "Go and sin no more."[174] But He did not punish her. Why?

4. It was sufficient for the woman what she encountered of humiliation, disgrace, and scandal. They set her in the midst, and they denounced her, saying, "This woman was caught in adultery, in the very act."[175] And with all cruelty they asked that the law should be applied on her, without applying the law on themselves.

---

172 John 8:7.
173 John 8:11.
174 Ibid.
175 John 8:4.

Therefore, the Lord gave them a lesson regarding their cruelty, their hypocrisy, their injustice in leaving the man [who was] committing adultery with her to escape unpunished.

5. As for the saying of that [writer who calls himself] Reader in his book, "According to human justice, Christ was not just," in this there is audacity and impudence against the Lord of glory. I wish he had risen, in meekness, above this manner of writing. There are other examples of his using this manner of speech; for example, his saying about the law, "It is not a knife in the hand of a cruel judge named God!"

The Parable of the Prodigal Son[176]

That writer [who calls himself Reader] used it as an example of free remission, without any punishment, even saying, "It was not mentioned that the father was harmed, nor did he show any displeasure whatsoever!" We cannot say that the father did not show any displeasure whatsoever. It was sufficient that he said to his servants, "For this my son was dead.... He was lost..."[177] and he said the same thing when speaking with the older brother, "For your brother was dead ... and was lost..."[178] So this indicates his displeasure with the behavior of the lost son, although he was joyful because he was alive after he was dead and was found after he was lost.

And concerning the joy of the father by the return of his son, that [writer who calls himself] Reader says in his book:

> Perhaps these words would put to shame the teaching of Anselm and all who claim that sin is considered dishonor directed against God, His justice, and His honor. And therefore, it is an infinite dishonor, for which God asks an infinite sacrifice of appeasement... of the teaching that gives off the stench of the Middle Ages!

---

176 Luke 15:11–32.
177 Luke 15:24.
178 Luke 15:31.

And thus he denies the bases of the teaching of divine redemption and the teaching of St. Athanasius! And he covers his denial of the teaching of the Church behind the words "Anselm" and the Middle Ages.

As for the words "put to shame" and "stench," we hope that he would rise above the use of such terms. As for his saying that sin is directed against God, and that it is infinite and needs an infinite sacrifice—these we will talk about and explain in the next article.

As for the joy of the father by the return of his son, this was not against the justice of God. For the justice of God ordains that repentance erases sin, and this son was repentant, and was even broken-hearted and had confessed his sins. God who said, "The soul who sins shall die,"[179] said in the same chapter, "But if a wicked man turns from all his sins which he has committed.... None of the transgressions which he has committed shall be remembered against him; because of the righteousness which he has done, he shall live."[180] He said on His forgiveness of the repentant, "For I will forgive their iniquity, and their sin I will remember no more."[181] This saying was preceded by His saying, "This is the covenant that I will make."[182] This resembles what He said in the Book of Isaiah, on the acceptance of the repentant that their sins "shall be as white as snow."[183] Therefore, the prodigal son, according to the Law, in his repentance was not deserving of any punishment, but was the object of the pleasure of the Lord.[184]

---

179 Ezekiel 18:20.
180 Ezekiel 18:21–22.
181 Jeremiah 31:34.
182 Jeremiah 31:33.
183 Isaiah 1:18.
184 See Ezekiel 18:23, 32.

CHAPTER SIX

The Meaning of "You Were Bought at a Price"

Introduction

It is clear that the Lord Christ has bought us by His blood, as it came in the following verses. "For you were bought at a price; therefore glorify God in your body and in your spirit, which are God's."[185] That is, you no longer own yourselves, but you are owned by the one who bought you. "You were bought at a price; do not become slaves of men."[186] "You are worthy to take the scroll, and to open its seals; for You were slain, and have redeemed[187] us to God by Your blood out of every tribe and tongue and people and nation."[188] "And no one could learn that song except the hundred and forty-four thousand who were redeemed[189] from the earth.... These were redeemed[190] from among men."[191] "Even denying the Lord who bought them."[192] This was said regarding the apostate.

St. Peter the Apostle, in another place, uses the word "redeemed"

---

185 1 Corinthians 6:20.
186 1 Corinthians 7:23.
187 The word in Arabic is "bought."
188 Revelation 5:9.
189 The word in Arabic is "bought."
190 Ibid.
191 Revelation 14:3–4.
192 2 Peter 2:1.

instead of "bought," carrying the same meaning, saying, "Knowing that you were not redeemed with corruptible things, like silver or gold ... but with the precious blood of Christ, as of a lamb without blemish and without spot."[193]

But the opponent tries to go into details, to complicate the matter, so he asks: Who is the buyer? And who is the seller?

Who is the buyer?

And it is natural that the buyer is our Lord Jesus Christ, who bought us by His blood, which is clear from the verse "for You were slain, and have redeemed[194] us to God by Your blood."[195] Regarding this St. Peter the Apostle says, "Knowing that you were not redeemed with corruptible things, like silver or gold ... but with the precious blood of Christ, as of a lamb without blemish and without spot."[196]

From whom did Christ buy us?

He bought us from death or the judgment of death. And we say the same thing in the Divine Liturgy According to St. Basil, "And, as a ransom on our behalf, [He] gave Himself up unto death, which reigned over us, whereby we were bound and sold on account of our sins."[197]

And concerning this St. Paul the Apostle says in his epistle to the Romans, "Therefore, just as through one man sin entered the world, and death through sin, and thus death spread to all men, because all sinned,"[198] adding, "Nevertheless death reigned from Adam..."[199] The Lord bought us from this death, which reigned over us because of our sins.

---

193 1 Peter 1:18–19.
194 The word in Arabic is "bought."
195 Revelation 5:9.
196 1 Peter 1:18–19.
197 The Divine Liturgy According to St. Basil – Agios (Holy).
198 Romans 5:12.
199 Romans 5:14.

Here comes the question: Who had sold us, that we were bought?

The [writer who calls himself] Reader mentions, quoting from one of his references, "If God had sold them, He sold them at no cost. And if He had recovered them, He recovered or released them at no cost too." We do not say that God sold us, as He did with the children of Israel when He delivered them to the hands of their enemies because of their sins. Rather, we say that man is the one who sold himself to death, because of his sins. For "the wages of sin is death,"[200] according to the Scripture. And as the Lord said, "The soul who sins shall die,"[201] and so "we were dead in trespasses."[202] The Lord Christ bought us by His blood from the judgment of death and granted us life.

The opponent, however, makes fun of this buying. [It seems that he is] as though he were making fun of the verses of the Holy Scriptures which indicate that we were bought by blood. So he says that the expressions of buying "do not harmonize with the words of psalmody: You made us gods, kings, and priests, and we will reign on the earth. For man can buy slaves and cattle, etc. but he cannot buy a king or a priest! Here we should understand that 'buying' here is 'acquiring.'"

And we wish that "this Reader" would have risen, in the theological research, above the comparison with buying slaves and cattle. But we say as an objective response the following. When the Lord bought us, we were not kings and priests, but we "were dead in trespasses and sins."[203] But we became kings and priests (spiritually) after He bought us by His blood, and by this blood He cleansed us from all sin,[204] and justified us and glorified us,[205] *then* He called us to be kings and priests. Then the kingship and spiritual priesthood were after He bought us by His blood, and not

---

200 Romans 6:23.
201 Ezekiel 18:4, 20.
202 Ephesians 2:5; also see Ephesians 2:1.
203 Ephesians 2:1.
204 See 1 John 1:7.
205 Romans 8:30.

before that. Rather, it was a result of this buying. And this is namely what came in the Book of Revelation, regarding this matter, "To Him who loved us and washed us from our sins in His own blood, and has made us kings and priests to His God and Father."[206]

And "the Reader" uses the same reverse reasoning, in which he uses "after" as it were "before," and he ["the Reader"] says, "And man is not bought [as] a temple of the Holy Spirit." And actually, when [that is, before] the Lord bought us, we were not temples of the Holy Spirit, but became so after He bought us and purified us by His blood from all sins.

As for the expression "acquiring" instead of "buying," how easy it is, in using this expression, to say that this acquisition came as a result of the buying. For a person acquires something by buying it. And the apostle's expression, "The church of God which He purchased[207] with His own blood,"[208] is not at all different from the expression "He bought it with His own blood," and the following expressions are integrated with it: "You were bought at a price,"[209] and "not redeemed with corruptible things, like silver or gold … but with the precious blood of Christ, as of a lamb without blemish and without spot."[210]

Why would the explicit verses concerning our being bought by the blood of Christ be ignored and substituted with other expressions carrying the same meaning, if the purpose were sound?

To whom was the price paid?

After this point, another arises: If God bought us by His blood, to whom was the price paid?

He answers, quoting one of his references, "The price was paid to us." "The blood which Christ offered [as] a price and ransom, He paid to no one but us." His same reference says, "The proper

---

206 Revelation 1:5.
207 The Arabic word in the verse is "acquired."
208 Acts 20:28.
209 1 Corinthians 7:23.
210 1 Peter 1:18–19.

state of the ransom: the price is paid to us," and he justifies his statement, that the price with which the Lord bought us—that is His blood—"we drink It, and yet without cost."

And of course, there is a great difference between "paid to us" and "paid for our sakes." And these are theological matters that require precision of expression. Christ paid His blood for our sakes, for the sake of our salvation and redemption, for the sake of our justification and sanctification, for the sake of paying the debt that was on us.

It is not reasonable that the price is paid to us, and we are the debtors. The Lord spoke about our debts in the story of the woman who washed His feet with her tears and wiped them with the hair of her head. For He said to the Pharisee, who judged Him in his thoughts, "There was a certain creditor who had two debtors. One owed five hundred denarii, and the other fifty. And when they had nothing with which to repay, he freely forgave them both."[211] The statement "forgave them both" here means that their debts were transferred to the account of the crucified Redeemer, that He may pay on their behalf. So how is it said that the price was paid to the debtor who is unable to pay his debt? Rather we ought to say that the price was paid for the sake of saving him from his debt.

As for our drinking the blood of Christ in the Mystery of Holy Communion, this does not mean that we are taking one of our rights, or that Communion is our due reward[212] by virtue of redemption. Rather, Communion is only a grace granted to us; it is a gift, not a right. I reiterate and say that meticulousness in using words is absolutely imperative in theological terminology.

And [the fact that] this blood is given to us without price [or cost] on our end, does not mean that it is granted to us without conditions. And the condition of worthiness is necessary, as St. Paul the Apostle explained, saying that whoever partakes in an unworthy manner "will be guilty of the body and blood of the Lord,"[213] and

---

211 Luke 7:41–42.
212 Or: our merit.
213 1 Corinthians 11:27.

partakes "judgment to himself."²¹⁴ We persistently partake of the precious blood, out of need and as a remedy, and not as those having a right, the price having been paid to us that we may drink It without price [or cost]!

Communion needs humility of heart to the uttermost. In it [the Divine Liturgy], the officiating²¹⁵ priest says in The Prayer of Preparation, "You, O Lord, know my unworthiness and unpreparedness and my lack of meetness for this Your holy service, and I do not have the countenance to draw near and open my mouth before Your holy glory, but according to the multitude of Your tender mercies, pardon me, a sinner. And grant to me that I may find grace and mercy at this hour."²¹⁶ He also says, "Grant, O Lord, that our sacrifice may be accepted before You for my own sins and for the ignorance of Your people."²¹⁷

---

214 1 Corinthians 11:29.
215 Literally: one serving the Mystery.
216 The Divine Liturgy According to St. Basil – Offering of the Lamb: The Prayer of Preparation.
217 The Divine Liturgy According to St. Basil – Offering of the Lamb: The Prayer after Preparation.

CHAPTER SEVEN

Sin is Directed Against God

This principle is necessary for the doctrine of redemption. For as long as sin is directed against God, and God is infinite, then sin is infinite, and its punishment is infinite, and there is no deliverance from this punishment except [through] an infinite propitiation. And from here came the Incarnation and redemption.

As for those who deny that sin is directed against God, they consequently despise the principle of redemption and propitiation. Their belief, also, that sin is not directed against God leads them to heedlessness, and consequently they do not believe in the gravity of sin nor of its punishment.

David the prophet sinned against Bathsheba, for he committed adultery with her. He also sinned against her husband Uriah the Hittite and contrived the matter of killing him. But when Nathan the prophet explained to him the gravity of his sin, he did not say that he sinned against Uriah the Hittite nor against Bathsheba, but he said, "I have sinned against the Lord,"[218] confessing that his sin was directed against God. And this is what he said in Psalm 51, when he spoke to the Lord in a profound statement: "Against You, You only, have I sinned, and done this evil in Your sight."[219]

Another example is Joseph the righteous. When sin was offered to him by his master's wife, he rose above this matter, feeling its gravity, saying his famous statement: "How then can I do this great

---

218 2 Samuel 12:13.
219 Psalms 51:4.

wickedness, and sin against God?"[220]

As for David's sin, we see that Nathan says to David, "Why have you despised the commandment of the LORD, to do evil in His sight?"[221] Here then the sin committed by David is directed against God. But we [even] see God says to David, "Now therefore, the sword shall never depart from your house, because you have despised Me, and have taken the wife of Uriah the Hittite to be your wife."[222] How extremely terrifying this verse is, that the Lord says to David, "you have despised Me." Is there a sin directed against God more [evident] than [what] this statement [demonstrates]? So how is it said that sin is not directed against God? Likewise, the punishment was grave, [coming] from the mouth of God.

And in the speech of the Lord with Moses the prophet, after the people of Israel worshiped the golden calf, Moses the prophet interceded for the people, saying to the Lord, "Yet now, if You will forgive their sin—but if not, I pray, blot me out of Your book which You have written."[223] And the Lord said to Moses, "Whoever has sinned against Me, I will blot him out of My book."[224] And this is another proof from the mouth of God that sin is directed against Him.

We also see in the ten commandments which God commanded and wrote with His finger at first, that He says in the third commandment, "You shall not take the name of the LORD your God in vain, for the LORD will not hold him guiltless who takes His name in vain."[225] And here we see another sin directed against God, which is taking His name in vain, and for it there is a severe punishment. And the Lord Christ in the sermon on the mount spoke about this point also, so He commanded that people should not swear, neither by the name of God, nor even by heaven, for it

---

220   Genesis 39:9.
221   2 Samuel 12:9.
222   2 Samuel 12:10.
223   Exodus 32:32.
224   Exodus 32:33.
225   Exodus 20:7.

is God's throne; nor by earth, for it is His footstool.[226] For swearing in vain is a disparagement of the holy name of God. And He says in Isaiah the prophet, "And My name is blasphemed continually every day."[227] But [even] the Apostle says, "'The name of God is blasphemed among the Gentiles because of you,' as it is written."[228] And here we see a sin against God, and it is the blaspheming of His name, and another sin [accounted] for the one who caused it.

Sin in general is a disobedience to God, and rebellion against His kingdom, and man's indifference[229] to being in the presence of God who watches his works and says to him, "I know your works."[230] On the contrary, Elijah the prophet said, "As the LORD of hosts lives, before whom I stand."[231] Therefore, sin is a sin against God the Almighty[232], who sees and hears and knows [everything]. Sin also is the rejection of God, as He said, "They rejected Me, the Beloved, as a contemptible dead [Man]."[233] And as He said, "They have forsaken Me, the fountain of living waters, and hewn themselves cisterns—broken cisterns that can hold no water."[234] It is even a provocation of God to anger, and there are many verses concerning this. And sin is the forgetfulness of God's favor to us and the forgetfulness of His love for us.

What shall we say then about atheism, paganism, and polytheism? Are not all these sins directed against God? And what shall we say about the existentialists' ridicule and mockery of God, and they say that heaven exists for the birds and God, so let Him leave the earth for us?

Man also sins against God in the person of His children, as He said to these on the left, "For I was hungry and you gave Me no food;

---

226 See Matthew 5:34–35.
227 Isaiah 52:5.
228 Romans 2:24.
229 Or: insensibility.
230 Revelation 3:1.
231 1 Kings 18:15.
232 Or: Pantocrator.
233 Cf. Psalms 37:21 LXX, OSB.
234 Jeremiah 2:13.

I was thirsty and you gave Me no drink."[235] And He considered that the one who sins against those in need, sins against Him Himself. For Christ is the head, and all the believers are members of His body. And the sin against the unbelievers is a sin against God in His creation. But even when a believer sins against themselves, it is also a sin against God. For he who sins against his body sins against the temple of God where His Holy Spirit dwells.[236] The Scripture says, "If anyone defiles the temple of God, God will destroy him. For the temple of God is holy, which temple you are."[237] He who sins joins God's enemies and becomes an enemy of God and is in debt to God also. And we will continue this point later.

---

[235] Matthew 25:42.
[236] See 1 Corinthians 3:16.
[237] 1 Corinthians 3:17.

CHAPTER EIGHT

How was the Redemption of Humankind Accomplished?

As this subject is of utmost sensitivity, I will speak about it with all clarity, using specific doctrinal points, for the sake of the soundness of the teaching in the Church. In this we will rely on the Holy Scriptures, the sayings of the [Church] Fathers, Tradition of the Church, and Church rites, because of the gravity of this subject with respect to the Christian faith.

1. Man was condemned to death.

As the Holy Scripture says, "Therefore, just as through one man sin entered the world, and death through sin, and thus death spread to all men, because all sinned."[238] And it also says, "Death reigned.... By the one man's offense death reigned."[239] It was inevitable that man dies, for the judgment of God from the beginning was clear, that is, "You shall surely die."[240] Our mother Eve knew this judgment fully before she sinned.[241]

Thus, it was inevitable that man dies.

St. Athanasius the Apostolic says in *On the Incarnation of the Word*, "For God would not be true, if, when He had said we should

---

238 Romans 5:12.
239 Romans 5:14, 17.
240 Genesis 2:17.
241 See Genesis 3:3.

die, man died not."²⁴² And concerning the judgement of death, St. Gregory says in the Divine Liturgy about man, "I plucked for myself the sentence of death."²⁴³ And St. Paul the Apostle says in his epistle to the Romans, "The wages of sin is death."²⁴⁴

So what is to be done to deliver man from death?

2. The only solution to deliver man is the Incarnation and redemption,

Regarding this St. Athanasius says in *On the Incarnation of the Word*, "He takes to Himself a body capable of death, that it, by partaking of the Word Who is above all, might be worthy to die in the stead of all."²⁴⁵ He reiterates the phrase, "Death in the stead of all."

Then he says, "It was impossible for the Word to suffer death, being immortal, and Son of the Father; to this end He takes to Himself a body capable of death, that it, by partaking of the Word Who is above all, might be worthy to die in the stead of all, and might, because of the Word which was come to dwell in it, remain incorruptible."²⁴⁶

He also says, "Whence, by offering unto death the body He Himself had taken, as an offering and sacrifice free from any stain…"²⁴⁷ And he also said about the Word, "The Word of God naturally by offering His own temple and corporeal instrument for the life of all satisfied the debt by His death."²⁴⁸

This is the sound Patristic teaching on the death of the Lord for our redemption and instead of all, that He may pay the debt of all.

---

242 Athanasius *On the Incarnation of the Word* 6. In *Nicene and Post-Nicene Fathers: Second Series* 4, P. Schaff, ed. (Peabody, MA: Hendrickson Publishers, 2012), 39 (henceforth cited as NPNF²).
243 The Divine Liturgy According to St. Gregory – Agios [Holy].
244 Romans 6:23.
245 Athanasius *On the Incarnation of the Word* 9 (NPNF² 4:40).
246 Athanasius *On the Incarnation of the Word* 9 (NPNF² 4:40–41).
247 Athanasius *On the Incarnation of the Word* 9 (NPNF² 4:41).
248 Ibid.

3. This redemption through His death, the Lord Christ accomplished alone.

Concerning this the Lord said in the Book of Isaiah the prophet, "I have trodden the winepress alone, and from the peoples no one was with Me."[249] And St. Peter the Apostle says about the Lord Christ, "Nor is there salvation in any other, for there is no other name under heaven given among men by which we must be saved."[250]

No one died on our behalf, except Christ. Nor did we die on behalf of ourselves, because humanity is incapable of saving itself. And if men died, this would not be redemption, but it is what is due. It is not sufficient. And this is what St. Gregory says in the Divine Liturgy:

> Neither an angel nor an archangel, neither a patriarch nor a prophet, have You entrusted with our salvation, but You, without change, were incarnate and became man, and resembled us in everything, except for sin alone, and became for us a mediator with the Father.... You have reconciled the earthly with the heavenly.[251]

He also says, "You, O my Master, have turned for me the punishment into salvation."[252]

The focus in the redemption is on Christ alone.

4. Therefore, it is wrong to say that we share in His redemptive sufferings.

As for the statement "the fellowship of His sufferings,"[253] it means that we are fellows with Him in the sufferings of service and evangelism, in enduring tribulations, persecutions, and humiliations, as St. Paul the Apostle said, "We are hard-pressed on

---

249 Isaiah 63:3.
250 Acts 4:12.
251 The Divine Liturgy According to St. Gregory – Prayer of Reconciliation.
252 The Divine Liturgy According to St. Gregory – Agios [Holy].
253 Philippians 3:10.

every side, yet not crushed; we are perplexed, but not in despair; persecuted, but not forsaken."[254]

He also said:

> But in all things we commend ourselves as ministers of God: in much patience, in tribulations, in needs, in distresses, in stripes, ... in labors, in sleeplessness, in fasts; ... by honor and dishonor, by evil report and good report; as deceivers, and yet true; as unknown, and yet well known; as dying, and behold we live; ... as sorrowful, yet always rejoicing; as poor, yet making many rich; as having nothing, and yet possessing all things.[255]

In this and similar like it[256] we enter into the fellowship of His sufferings. As for His redemptive sufferings, we cannot share in them, for we do not share in the redemption—God forbid! We do not take the attribute of Christ as a redeemer and ascribe it to ourselves. And if we share in the redemptive sufferings, then the question is: Who are we redeeming?

5. Christ was crucified on our behalf, died on our behalf, and suffered on our behalf.

Very sadly, on the subject of the fellowship of the redemptive sufferings, some deny that Christ was crucified on our behalf, died on our behalf, and suffered on our behalf. And on this he literally says:

> Christ was crucified then not alone, but we were crucified with Him. So how do we say that He was crucified on our behalf? And when Christ died, He did not die alone, but we died with Him. So how do we say that He died on our behalf? And we have previously said that we suffered with Him. So how do we say that He suffered on our behalf?

---

254 2 Corinthians 4:8–9.
255 2 Corinthians 6:4–10.
256 See 2 Corinthians 11.

The writer, who has this thought, uses the following excuse: "The sacrifice of Christ is death of the sinner in actuality! Christ took a body which is in its truth a body of man as a whole, the body of all sinners… It is the selfsame body of every sinner… so that every sinner may consider himself to have actually died in Christ." "The body of our humankind, that is the body of every single one of men." "He died in our body, in our blood, and in our flesh."

We would like to discuss all these statements.

6. Did Christ die in the body of all humankind, in the body of all sinners, in the body of every sinner?

The theological truth, which I would like to say, so that the matter may not become confusing for the reader, is the following:

Christ was crucified, died, and suffered in a human body, and not in the body of all humankind, not in the body of all sinners; rather, in a single body, pure and without blemish. Therefore, when His blood was shed on our behalf to redeem us, it was as St. Peter the Apostle said, "Knowing that you were not redeemed with corruptible things … but with the precious blood of Christ, as of a lamb without blemish and without spot."[257]

It is impossible for Christ to unite with the body of all sinners. For according to Scripture: "And what communion has light with darkness? And what accord has Christ with Belial?"[258] And it is impossible for the body of sinners to ascend the cross, uniting with Christ. For the offering which is offered [as] a sacrifice to God should be without blemish, and this is the scriptural teaching of both the Old and New Testaments. As for humankind, it was said of it, "They have all turned aside, they have together become corrupt; there is none who does good, no, not one,"[259] "for all have sinned and fall short of the glory of God."[260] And St. John the Apostle said, "If we say that we have no sin, we deceive ourselves,

---

257 1 Peter 1:18–19.
258 2 Corinthians 1:14–15.
259 Psalms 14:3.
260 Romans 3:23.

and the truth is not in us."[261]

So how do you offer on the cross sinful bodies, with which Christ unites, who is alone without sin, of whom it was said to His mother the Virgin when He was incarnate, "that Holy One who is to be born will be called the Son of God"[262]?

7. The redemption of the body of all sinners was not accomplished on the cross.

Another point should be added to what was previously said: The redemption of the body of all sinners was not accomplished on the cross. Those whose redemption was accomplished are they who believed and who repented, and not all, although the sacrifice of Christ is sufficient to bear the sins of the whole world. But no one benefits from it, except those who believed and repented, and who were baptized also.

Concerning those who believed, the Scripture says, "For God so loved the world that He gave His only begotten Son, that whoever believes in Him should not perish but have everlasting life."[263] It also says, "He who believes in the Son has everlasting life; and he who does not believe the Son shall not see life, but the wrath of God abides on him."[264] It is likewise in John 3:18.

Then those who do not believe are not of the redeemed. And likewise, those who did not repent, according to the saying of the Lord: "Unless you repent you will all likewise perish."[265] And concerning Baptism, the Scripture says, "He who believes and is baptized will be saved."[266]

So how is it said, in the operation of redemption, that Christ united with the body of all sinners, while some of them were not redeemed? From all, did He unite with the body of Judas, whom

---

261 1 John 1:8.
262 Luke 1:35.
263 John 3:16.
264 John 3:36.
265 Luke 13:3, 5.
266 Mark 16:16.

He described as the son of perdition? And did He unite with Annas and Caiaphas, Pilate, Nero, and Diocletian, who are all included in the statement "all sinners"?

8. "For us"[267] or "for our sakes"

There is another statement that requires analysis. This is the expression "for us" or "for our sakes." It is marvelous that the matter is depicted as "a grave matter" or "a theological error," while the Holy Scriptures use both expressions, and so do the Divine Liturgy and the Orthodox Creed. So, is it said to people that the error encompasses all these?

The writer says, "It is erroneous to say, 'crucified for us,' but 'crucified for our sakes.' And it is erroneous to say, 'died for us,' but 'died for our sakes.' And it is erroneous to say, 'suffered for us,' but 'suffered for our sakes.'"

It is evident that all of us use these expressions which he describes as "theological error." In **the Orthodox Creed**, we say, "And He was crucified for us under Pontius Pilate," and not for our sakes. So, is there an error in which all believers fall in reciting the Orthodox Creed?

In **the Holy Scriptures**, the Lord says in the Gospel of Luke, "This cup is the new covenant in My blood, which is shed for you."[268] So the writer says, "Here the translation in Arabic is wrong," and he quotes what came in Matthew 26 and Mark 14, that it is "shed for the sake of many."[269] So, what do we say then about the saying of the Lord in the Gospels of Matthew and Mark that "the Son of Man did not come to be served, but to serve, and to give His life a ransom for many."[270] So, is there an error in the

---

267 Or: on our behalf.
268 Luke 22:20.
269 This is translated from Arabic. NKJV translation of the verses in question all agree and do not have "for the sake." Here are the verses:
"'This is My blood of the new covenant, which is shed for many" (Mark 14:24). "For this is My blood of the new covenant, which is shed for many for the remission of sins" (Matthew 26:28).
270 Matthew 20:28 and Mark 10:45.

translation of these two gospels too, as he said about the Gospel of Luke (22:20). And what is the point in confusing the minds concerning the three Gospels?

In **the Divine Liturgy**, the following came, "He loved His own who were in the world, and, as a ransom on our behalf, gave Himself up unto death."[271] Is there an error in the Divine Liturgy too? And also in the Divine Liturgy, "For being determined to give Himself up to death for the life of the world, He took bread..."[272] Is this wrong too?

And the saying of the Lord, "For this is My Body, which is broken for you and for many, to be given for the remission of sins.... For this is My Blood of the New Covenant, which is shed for you and for many, to be given for the remission of sins."[273] Is this wrong also?

And in The Confession in the Divine Liturgy, we say about the Body of the Lord, "He gave It up for us upon the holy wood of the Cross, of His own will, for us all." Is all this wrong, knowing that it came in all three Liturgies according to St. Basil, St. Gregory and St. Cyril?

St. Athanasius uses the expressions, "to die in the stead of all,"[274] and "by offering His own temple and corporeal instrument for the life of all,"[275] and, "should avail for all."[276]

Why all this commotion around the term "for us"? The author says, "Because the word 'for us' here is extremely grave, for it makes death and the curse as a personal due[277]. And this cancels the ransom completely." No, there is no gravity, for the personal due belongs to us ourselves, but the Redeemer bore it for us.

---

271 The Divine Liturgy According to St. Basil – Agios [Holy].
272 The Divine Liturgy According to St. Basil – The Institution Narrative.
273 Ibid.
274 Athanasius *On the Incarnation of the Word* 9 (NPNF² 4:40).
275 Athanasius *On the Incarnation of the Word* 9 (NPNF² 4:41).
276 Athanasius *On the Incarnation of the Word* 9 (NPNF² 4:40).
277 Or: worthiness.

9. The writer says, "We were crucified with Him and died with Him."[278]

And he continues, saying, "For He did not die far from us, but died in our body, our blood, and our flesh. For we are partakers *in* this body and blood…" And he says that "the death of redemption which Christ died is our death;" "The sacrifice of Christ is death of the sinner in actuality;" "He did not die alone on the cross, for we were in Him on the cross—'I have been crucified with Christ;'" "And when He was buried, we were buried with Him;" "And His resurrection is our resurrection."

We note in the term "died with Him" that there is confusion between the cross and Baptism. And likewise [is the case] for the term "We were buried with Him." For we did not die with Christ on the cross of Golgotha and were not buried with Him in the tomb which Joseph of Arimathea prepared for Him! But the Apostle says, "Or do you not know that as many of us as were baptized into Christ Jesus were baptized into His death? Therefore we were buried with Him through baptism."[279] And he affirms the same meaning in the epistle to the Colossians, saying, "[You were] buried with Him in baptism, in which you also were raised with Him."[280] Then we, in Baptism, die with Christ and rise with Him, and we do not die with Him on the cross of Golgotha, nor do we rise from the tomb in which He was buried.

Therefore, we find that the Apostle in the same chapter in the epistle to the Romans says, "If we have been united together in the likeness of His death, certainly we also shall be in the likeness of His resurrection."[281] And the Apostle continues, saying, "Knowing this, that our old man was crucified with Him."[282] All this is about Baptism, and not the cross of Golgotha. And when Paul the Apostle says, "I have been crucified with Christ,"[283] he does not mean that

---

278 See Romans 6:8.
279 Romans 6:3–4.
280 Colossians 2:12.
281 Romans 6:5.
282 Romans 6:6.
283 Galatians 2:20.

he was crucified with Him on the mount of Golgotha. For at that time he was not a believer, but he said about himself, "Although I was formerly a blasphemer, a persecutor, and an insolent man; but I obtained mercy because I did it ignorantly in unbelief."[284]

It is not permitted that verses are taken and used in a different context[285]. For Paul the Apostle was saying, at that time, that he was justified by faith and not the Law. Therefore, he said after that, "Christ lives in me; and the life which I now live in the flesh I live by faith."[286]

And here I would like to ask a question about confusing between the cross and Baptism: If we had died on the cross with Christ, having been crucified with Him, so why is Baptism necessary then? Is it to die and to be crucified again? And if we died with Him in Baptism, and our old man was crucified in Baptism, then we had not died before that with Him nor in Him. Otherwise, we would have died twice and have been crucified twice. Therefore, the Apostle, with the expression "died with Him,"[287] uses the expression "in the likeness of His death."[288]

Likewise, the statements, "For Your sake we are killed all day long,"[289] and, "Always carrying about in the body the dying of the Lord Jesus,"[290] and, "For we who live are always delivered to death"[291]—all these do not at all mean death with Him on the cross. For the terms "all day long" and "always" do not apply to the death of the cross. Rather, they are all taken with the spiritual meaning with respect to suffering pain because of the Christian faith, or mortifications in the spiritual struggle, or crucifying the flesh along with the passions[292]. And another like it is: "Therefore,

---

284 1 Timothy 1:13.
285 Literally: used in a place not theirs.
286 Galatians 2:20.
287 See Romans 6:8.
288 Romans 6:5.
289 Romans 8:36.
290 2 Corinthians 4:10.
291 2 Corinthians 4:11.
292 See Galatians 5:24.

if you died with Christ from the basic principles of the world, why, as though living in the world?"²⁹³ Again, how dangerous it is to use verses out of context!

10. Was the redemption accomplished by the blood of Christ alone, or by the blood of all of us?

Commenting on the statement, "[He] died in our body, our blood, and our flesh," was the redemption accomplished by the blood of Christ alone, or by the blood of all of us?

Look, the Scriptures emphasize on the blood of Christ alone, saying:

"[We] having now been justified by His blood."²⁹⁴

"…a propitiation by His blood, through faith."²⁹⁵

"In Him we have redemption through His blood, the forgiveness of sins."²⁹⁶

"… but with the precious blood of Christ, as of a lamb without blemish and without spot."²⁹⁷

"And the blood of Jesus Christ His Son cleanses us from all sin."²⁹⁸

"… the church of God which He purchased with His own blood."²⁹⁹

As for the statement "our body, our blood, and our flesh," it does not exist [in the Holy Scriptures]. It also diminishes of the value of the ransom of Christ, who died alone for our sakes, who has "trodden the winepress alone, and from the peoples no one was with Me."³⁰⁰ Also, humankind, in the expression "our blood and

---

293 Colossians 2:20.
294 Romans 5:9.
295 Romans 3:25.
296 Ephesians 1:7.
297 1 Peter 1:18–19.
298 1 John 1:7.
299 Acts 20:28.
300 Isaiah 63:3.

our flesh," thinks of itself more highly than it ought to[301]. Another point we would like to add to the previous article is the following.

11. Was the sacrifice of Christ a sacrifice of love or punishment?

The purpose of this question is to confuse the people's minds, like discussing "for us or for our sakes." For the matter is very clear: The sacrifice of Christ was [out of] love for us *and* a payment[302] of the punishment which was on us, that is, the judgment of death. So, it joined the two matters together.

But a certain writer says, "God gave His Son out of His love for the world, that the world may not perish… There is here not the least likelihood in the existence of punishment;" "there is no sense of punishment in the least." Then the writer says about the Lord Christ: "But His death in our body was accounted to us as a payment of the punishment. For when He fulfilled the death, He fulfilled His love. For it belongs to us to fulfill the punishment. As for Him, by death He fulfilled His love."

Then there is punishment, but Christ bore it on our behalf, because of His love for us. Otherwise, what is the meaning of "payment of the punishment" and "fulfill the punishment"? Who paid the punishment, except the Lord Christ? And who fulfilled the punishment, except the Lord Christ? All of this was instead of us. For as the Scripture says, "All we like sheep have gone astray; we have turned, every one, to his own way; and the LORD has laid on Him the iniquity of us all."[303] And because of "the iniquity of us all," the Lord Christ suffered, died, and was buried.

Otherwise, why did He die? Except that there was a punishment decreed against us. But the writer says, "If death had been the punishment of sin—and it is truly so in the Old Testament: 'The soul who sins shall die'[304]—the Son would have borne the

---

301 See Romans 12:3.
302 Or: satisfaction.
303 Isaiah 53:6.
304 Ezekiel 18:20.

punishment of death from the hand of the Father in our place, to satisfy the justice of God. And this is foreign to the spirit of the New Testament and is inadmissible."

12. Is there disagreement between the Old and New Testaments?

And here we ask, "Is there disagreement between the Old and New Testaments?" God, as the Scriptures say, "is the same yesterday, today, and forever,"[305] "with whom there is no variation or shadow of turning."[306]

If, in the Old Testament, "the soul who sins shall die,"[307] the same judgment is in the New Testament too. We see this in the story of Ananias and Sapphira,[308] in the end of Judas "the son of perdition,"[309] in the plagues of the Book of Revelation, and in the first epistle of John, where he says, "There is sin leading to death. I do not say that he should pray about that."[310]

As for the statement "the Son would have borne the punishment of death from the hand of the Father in our place, to satisfy the justice of God," this is not foreign to the spirit of the New Testament as the writer says. Rather it is the belief of the whole Church and the belief of her fathers and saints.

The writer continues in his opinion, saying, "It is impossible that the Father gathers in His heart the vengeance of the punishment, that He may pour it onto His Son to die for us and instead of us!" So does this agree with the saying of the Scripture, "And the LORD has laid on Him the iniquity of us all"[311]? And does it agree with the saying of the Scripture, "Yet it pleased the LORD to bruise Him;

---

305 Hebrews 13:8.
306 James 1:17.
307 Ezekiel 18:20.
308 See Acts 5.
309 John 17:12.
310 1 John 5:16.
311 Isaiah 53:6.

He has put Him to grief,"[312] and that "He was numbered with the transgressors"[313]?

13. Is death a punishment according to the teaching of the Scripture, or not?

From the beginning of humankind, God warned Adam about this punishment of death. And He said to him concerning eating of the tree, "You shall surely die."[314] Eve confirmed her knowledge of this punishment.[315] And the writer confesses that the punishment of sin is death in the Old Testament, according to Ezekiel (18:20).

The New Testament also confirmed that the punishment of sin is death. It came in Romans that "the wages of sin is death,"[316] and, "and thus death spread to all men, because all sinned."[317] And in Ephesians, he says, "[You] who were dead in trespasses and sins..."[318] And the Master Lord, in His letter to the church in Thyatira in the Book of Revelation, says concerning Jezebel the sinner, "I will kill her children with death."[319]

Therefore, if death were the punishment of sin, and the Lord Christ is Holy [and] without sin, then why did He die? There is no reason but that He died for us and bore the punishment of sin instead of us. And this is the redemption.

14. The sufferings of Christ for us and His redemptive death for us, are [at] the depth of the rites of the Church in Holy Week.

The sufferings of Christ for us are the reason[320] for our mourning

---

312   Isaiah 53:10.
313   Isaiah 53:12.
314   Genesis 2:17.
315   See Genesis 3:3.
316   Romans 6:23.
317   Romans 5:12.
318   Ephesians 2:1.
319   Revelation 2:23.
320   Literally: secret, mystery.

tunes during Holy Pascha Week, are the reason for the black drapery with which the church is covered, are the reason for all the readings and prophecies which we read, and are the reason for our profound fasting in this week.

And in all this, we bring to remembrance that cup which the Lord drank, and [though] we were ourselves deserving of drinking it. For we are the ones deserving of the sufferings, crucifixion, and death—and not He. But He, out of His exceeding love for us, endured all that instead of us. He bore our sins and He is holy, and bore our punishment and He is innocent. And the Father hid His face from Him, [yet] His face was supposed to be hid from us ourselves.

If the matter were love only, with not even the least likelihood of the existence of punishment in it (as the writer says)—Yes, if the matter were love only, Holy [Passion] Week in the church would have turned into Joyful Week with joyful tunes. But the love of Christ for us was manifest in His enduring the punishment instead of us. His love is inseparable from the thorns, nails, and the cross. And His love for us was the reason for His enduring the shame and mockery which befit us, "despising the shame."[321] This is what we mention in our Divine Liturgies, saying to Him:

> You have borne the oppression of the wicked. You have given Your back to the scourge. Your cheeks You have left open to those who smite. For my sake, O my Master, You have not hidden Your face from the shame of spitting.[322]

Do we forget all this and say that the cross is entirely love only? And in our enjoyment of love, we forget our punishment and this Lover who bore it for us[323].

15. Was the story of the cross then bereft of punishment?

---

321 Hebrews 12:2.
322 The Divine Liturgy According to St. Gregory – Agios [Holy].
323 Or: on our behalf.

The writer says, "And this is the fundamental mystery in the Incarnation of the Son of God, that it is foremost a work of love, completely far away from the sense and concept of punishment. For neither did the Father punish His Son, but out of love delivered Him up; nor did the Son punish Himself, but He loved us and delivered Himself for our sakes; nor did a punishment fall upon us in truth, but we won exoneration, love, and adoption."

O our joy in this alleged exoneration, in which we forget all our sins and iniquities and uncleanness, and forget all the suffering and shame which we caused our Redeemer!

Also, we did not win exoneration, not at all, but rather what we won is that we were not condemned. For if we had not been condemned to the highest degree, if we had not been dead in trespasses and sins,[324] if we had not been deserving of punishment—if not all that, Christ would not have been crucified, nor would His sufferings have taken place. Is it because on Christ the Redeemer was laid "the iniquity of us all,"[325] that we are without iniquity, and we win exoneration? Is it to this extent that sinners forget their sins, which the loving Redeemer bore on their behalf, and say, "We have won exoneration"? Is it the focusing on the self—our selves which the Redeemer saved by His death—while forgetting the sufferings which the Savior endured and the high price which He paid on our behalf?

The mystery of the Incarnation of the Son of God is not far from the sense and concept of punishment. For had it not been for the punishment which was on us, He would not have become incarnate. The fundamental reason for the Incarnation is the redemption, and the reason for the redemption is saving us from our punishment.

And so, in announcing the conception of Christ to Joseph the carpenter, it was said to him, "And you shall call His name JESUS, for He will save His people from their sins."[326] He was born then to

---

324 See Ephesians 2:1.
325 Isaiah 53:6.
326 Matthew 1:21.

be a Savior, saving the believers from the punishment of their sins. The same meaning is what the angels said in announcing to the shepherds, "I bring you good tidings of great joy which will be to all people. For there is born to you this day in the city of David a Savior, who is Christ the Lord."[327]

Then salvation is the reason for the Incarnation. Salvation is that the Lord Christ saves us from the punishment of our sins, from the death that reigned over us, whereby we were bound and sold on account of our sins, as we say in the Divine Liturgy. For if it had not been for the punishment of death, which reigned over all because of sin,[328] if it had not been for the redemption from this death, the Incarnation would have taken place, nor the crucifixion. So, how is it said then that the Incarnation is completely far away from the sense and concept of punishment? These words are completely far away from the teaching of the Scripture and the teaching of the Fathers.

16. The relationship of the Father with the Son in the crucifixion

The statement "the Father punished His Son" is a provocative statement, for the Son was not a sinner that the Father may punish Him. But the correct statement is that the Father accepted that His Son bears the punishment that was on humankind. And so He sent Him "to be the propitiation for our sins."[329] And the statement "out of love delivered Him up," we do not easily pass over. Rather we stop at "He delivered," that is, He delivered Him up to death and crucifixion, and delivered Him up "an offering for sin,"[330] that "He was numbered with the transgressors."[331] And He delivered Him up wounded for our transgressions and bruised for our iniquities,[332]

---

327 Luke 2:10–11.
328 See Romans 5:12, 14.
329 1 John 4:10.
330 Isaiah 53:10.
331 Isaiah 53:12.
332 See Isaiah 53:5.

"yet we esteemed Him stricken, smitten by God, and afflicted."[333] And He "has laid on Him the iniquity of us all. He was oppressed and He was afflicted, yet He opened not His mouth; He was led as a lamb to the slaughter, and as a sheep before its shearers is silent, so He opened not His mouth."[334]

Do we pass over all this easily and say, "out of love He delivered Him up"? It is true that the Father loved us and sent His Son to be the propitiation for our sins. But what does all this mean? What is the meaning behind the terms? It is sufficient that we put before us the following verses, which clearly express the Father's position toward the Son on the subject of the cross:

"He who did not spare His own Son, but delivered Him up for us all."[335] This verse gives meaning to the term "He delivered Him up."

"Yet it pleased the LORD to bruise Him; He has put Him to grief,"[336] And I wish that we meditate on the terms "bruise Him" and "grief" here, adding to them, "He was bruised for our iniquities"[337]

[Consider] the saying of the Lord Christ on the cross, "My God, My God, why have You forsaken Me?"[338] and His saying also in the garden of Gethsemane, "O My Father, if this cup cannot pass away from Me unless I drink it, Your will be done."[339] and His saying before that, "Shall I not drink the cup which My Father has given Me?"[340]

All these statements require deep meditation, that we may understand that the Father forsaking Him is not a forsaking of separation—certainly not!—but forsaking Him to suffering, that He may drink the entire cup with all the suffering and shame it contains. And the Father was pleased by this, that the price of sin

---

333 Isaiah 53:4.
334 Isaiah 53:6–7.
335 Romans 8:32.
336 Isaiah 53:10.
337 Isaiah 53:5.
338 Mark 15:34.
339 Matthew 26:42.
340 John 18:11.

was fully paid, body and soul: the suffering of the body and the bitterness of soul.

17. The sufferings of the Son in the operation of redemption

We move on to the statement "nor did the Son punish Himself, but He loved us and delivered Himself for our sakes." And the expression "the Son punished Himself" is neither acceptable theologically nor spiritually. For it carries the meaning of suicide, and this without a reason. It is more acceptable to say: The sufferings of the Son in the operation of redemption.

This is made clear in the prophecies in Psalm 22, which concerns the sufferings of Christ. At the beginning, it says, "My God, My God, why have You forsaken Me?"[341] Some meditate that the Lord Christ, when He said this statement on the cross, intended to direct people's eyes to what was said about Him in this psalm. Of that: "They pierced My hands and My feet; I can count all My bones,"[342] and, "They divide My garments among them, and for My clothing they cast lots."[343]

In this psalm also: "All those who see Me ridicule Me; they shoot out the lip, they shake the head, saying, 'He trusted in the LORD, let Him rescue Him; let Him deliver Him, since He delights in Him!'"[344] "I am poured out like water, and all My bones are out of joint; My heart is like wax; it has melted within Me. My strength is dried up like a potsherd, and My tongue clings to My jaws."[345] "Many bulls have surrounded Me; strong bulls of Bashan have encircled Me."[346]

To all these sufferings is added the scourging, nails, [crown of] thorns, the ridicules, spitting, and reproaches. And the prophecy

---

341 Psalms 22:1.
342 Psalms 22:16–17.
343 Psalms 22:18.
344 Psalms 22:7–8.
345 Psalms 22:14–15.
346 Psalms 22:12.

concerning Him, "And for my thirst they gave me vinegar to drink,"[347] was fulfilled: "They gave Him sour wine mingled with gall to drink."[348] And out of the severity of His exertion on the cross, He said, "I thirst!"[349]

All this and more can be expressed easily or ignored with the expression "But He loves us and delivered Himself for our sakes." What does "delivered Himself" carry? Delivered Himself up to what? To the purple robe and being struck on the face, and saying to Him, "Prophesy! Who is the one who struck You?"[350] and "Hail, King of the Jews!"[351]? Or the prophecy concerning Him: "I gave My back to those who struck Me, and My cheeks to those who plucked out the beard; I did not hide My face from shame and spitting."[352] Do we forget all this and only remember the expression "He loved us and delivered Himself"? And what did He pay for the sake of that love?

Do we after all this say that all that happened was completely far away from the sense and concept of punishment? Were not we ourselves deserving of all that Christ gave [i.e. suffered] for our sakes? Or do we only think of ourselves and say, "He loved us" and "we won exoneration," and do not think of that crucified Lover, nor the punishment which He bore instead of us?

18. Did Christ bear the punishment, or annul the punishment?

There is another point, which may appear intuitive, but we are obliged to present it, which is: Did Christ bear the punishment, or annul the punishment? The writer says, "Punishment does not generate love, but love annuls the punishment." By this he as though sees that all the punishments with which God punished

---

347 Psalms 69:21.
348 Matthew 27:34.
349 John 19:28.
350 Luke 22:64.
351 Matthew 27:29.
352 Isaiah 50:6.

the world in the Old and New Testaments were bereft of love. But the Scripture says, "For whom the LORD loves He chastens, and scourges every son whom He receives."[353]

Then the writer addressed the punishment which Christ bore instead of us, saying, "For how can we say afterwards that Christ, by His death, bore the punishment for us? What is correct is that by His death He annulled the punishment, for His death was out of God's love, and not a punishment."

If Christ did not bear the punishment for us, what would be the meaning of the redemption then? And if there were not a punishment at all—through the annulment of the punishment!—where would then be the satisfaction of divine justice? Did the Christ suffer and die for no reason? The reason for the lifting up of the punishment from us was that Christ bore it instead of us. And this is the teaching of the Church throughout the ages and the teaching of the Scripture.

19. Who fulfilled the divine justice, we or Christ?

And this drags us to a marvelous point which the writer raises, which is: Who fulfilled the divine justice, we or Christ? This is a marvelous question which the saying of the writer raises: "For Christ died in the body, which is our body, and our sin is on Him. So, the justice of God was fulfilled in us ourselves, and not in Christ." This statement calls for astonishment, and it leads to the destruction of the entire doctrine of redemption!

If the justice of God was fulfilled in us, what then did Christ do? Why was He incarnate? Why did He suffer, die, and why was He buried? And what is the meaning of His title "Savior" who saves His people from their sins, and what was the point of naming Him "Jesus"?

As for "He died in our body," our body is sinful and is not fit to be offered a sacrifice. But Christ died in a pure body "as of a lamb

---

353 Hebrews 12:6.

without blemish and without spot."[354] Having no sin, He died for the sin of another, for the sins of the whole world.

The foundation of redemption is that man was utterly incapable of saving himself, incapable of paying his debts before the divine justice, as the Lord said about the debtors who owed one fifty and another five hundred denarii, "And when they had nothing with which to repay, he freely forgave them both."[355] And how did he forgive them? The Scripture says, "…in whom we have redemption through His blood, the forgiveness of sins."[356]

20. Did Christ die by His will, or merely in obedience to the Father? And is He the Redeemer, or the Ransom?

Some try to destroy the work of Christ in the redemption, either by making men share in the work of redemption, that we ourselves fulfilled the requirement of God's justice; or by focusing on the work of God the Father, that He is the Redeemer, and that Christ is merely a ransom the Father offered. But the Son "became obedient to the point of death, even the death of the cross."[357]

Numerous are the verses that say that Christ is the one who redeemed us, and we will mention here few verses showing that He offered Himself, gave Himself for us, and laid Himself down.

"I lay down My life that I may take it again. No one takes it from Me, but I lay it down of Myself. I have power to lay it down, and I have power to take it again."[358]

"The Man Christ Jesus, who gave Himself a ransom for all."[359]

"He poured out His soul unto death."[360]

"[Christ] who gave Himself for us, that He might redeem us

---

354 1 Peter 1:19.
355 Luke 7:42.
356 Colossians 1:14.
357 Philippians 2:8.
358 John 10:17–18.
359 1 Timothy 2:5–6.
360 Isaiah 53:12.

from every lawless deed."[361]

"[Christ] who gave Himself for our sins, that He might deliver us from this present evil age."[362]

21. The Lord Christ laid Himself down, gave Himself for us, and delivered Himself to death, that He may redeem us and save us.

Concerning the role which the Lord Christ did in the redemption of men, we would like to present some verses that indicate the following truth: The Lord Christ laid Himself down, gave Himself for us, and delivered Himself to death, that He may redeem us and save us.

For the writer says, "The Father is the Redeemer, and the Son is the Ransom. Therefore, the title redeemer, with respect to Christ, did not come in all the books of the New Testament, and this is out of theological awareness, which is precise and eye-catching. For the Father is He who has the everlasting counsel and the economy in offering His Son a ransom."

Although we do not presently desire to go into the theological relationship between the Father and the Son in such matters, and although the writer himself says, in the same book, few pages later, "The Redeemer calls you: Look at My wounds and the sin which I bore, and the curse which I accepted…" and he means Christ, of course, but I would like to prove that Christ has redeemed us, by His will and His pleasure, and not merely in obedience to the Father, that "[He] became obedient to the point of death, even the death of the cross."[363] For this was said concerning His humanity, but the Divinity does not die, and Christ died in the flesh. And "obedience" here means the agreement of the will.

22. The Lord Christ Himself made this truth clear.

---

361 Titus 2:14.
362 Galatians 1:4.
363 Philippians 2:8.

This is by saying about Himself, "I lay down My life that I may take it again.... I have power to lay it down, and I have power to take it again."[364]

He also said in the same chapter, "I am the good shepherd. The good shepherd gives His life for the sheep,"[365] and after that He said, "I lay down My life for the sheep."[366]

He also said, "The bread that I shall give is My flesh, which I shall give for the life of the world."[367] Then He gives Himself, and He is not merely given.

And so we say in the Divine Liturgy, "For being determined to give Himself up to death for the life of the world."[368] That is, this was by His will and His plan, that He gives Himself up for the life of the world. And He fully knows that for this reason He came to the world.

23. The Apostles also confirm this truth.

"[Christ] who gave Himself for our sins, that He might deliver us from this present evil age."[369] He said, "He gave Himself" and not "He was given."

"[The Son of God] who loved me and gave Himself for me."[370]

"Christ also has loved us and given Himself for us, an offering and a sacrifice to God for a sweet-smelling aroma."[371]

"[He] who through the eternal Spirit offered Himself without spot to God."[372]

And the Apostle says about the Church and her relationship

---

364 John 10:17–18.
365 John 10:11.
366 John 10:15.
367 John 6:51.
368 The Divine Liturgy According to St. Basil – The Institution Narrative.
369 Galatians 1:4.
370 Galatians 2:20.
371 Ephesians 5:2.
372 Hebrews 9:14.

with Christ, "Just as Christ also loved the church and gave Himself for her, that He might sanctify and cleanse her with the washing of water by the word."[373]

"He laid down His life for us."[374]

24. The Lord Christ is the one who redeemed us.

The Apostle says, "Christ has redeemed us from the curse of the law,"[375] and did not say that the Father is the one who redeemed us.

And he says about the Christ, "In Him we have redemption through His blood, the forgiveness of sins, according to the riches of His grace."[376]

"Being justified freely by His grace through the redemption that is in Christ Jesus."[377]

"[Christ] who gave Himself a ransom for all."[378]

Christ then redeemed us, gave Himself up, and justified us freely by His redemption of us, and by His blood we received remission of sins. And He offered Himself to death.

25. In the omission of the will of Christ in the redemption, there is a diminution of His love for us.

The one who says that Christ is not the Redeemer but is merely a ransom the Father offered, and He accepted that for the sake of obedience, diminishes the love of Christ for us and His giving Himself up for the sake of the forgiveness of our sins.

It is impossible that the Church accepts this matter, of which the Apostle said, "Just as Christ also loved the church and gave

---

373 Ephesians 5:25–26.
374 1 John 3:16.
375 Galatians 3:13.
376 Ephesians 1:7.
377 Romans 3:24.
378 1 Timothy 2:6.

Himself for her."[379] But this matter is not accepted by any one of us, for we say with the Apostle about the Lord Christ, "Who loved me and gave Himself for me."[380] Christ was not merely the executioner of the Father's will in the redemption, for the sake of obedience, but His will was itself the will of the Father concerning the redemption.

26. There is a great difference between the words "theory" and "doctrine."

We all believe that redemption is that a person[381] redeems another, by taking his place, dying on his behalf, and paying the price instead of him. But someone comes up with an opinion and says, "There are three theories of redemption: Substitutionary theory, the satisfaction of the Father theory, and the ransom theory by paying the price."

And the matter turns, in his explanation, from doctrine to theories he discusses, as though the [Church] Fathers have not left us a firm doctrine on the subject of redemption. And the matter develops into a declaration that [the idea] that a soul takes the place for a soul prevailed in the Old Testament, but the matter has changed in the New Testament, and union now took the place of substitution.

Why do you remove the ancient landmarks so quickly? Why the attack against the saintly Early Fathers in what they have offered of doctrine? And why introduce a new belief, which obliges us to protect the people from? Did the Scripture not say, "Do not remove the ancient landmark which your fathers have set"[382]? Why all this confusion and the attempt at overturning what the Church has received through many past generations, through firm traditions?

27. "Pleasing[383] the heart of God"

---

379 Ephesians 5:25.
380 Galatians 2:20.
381 Or: soul.
382 Proverbs 22:28.
383 Or: satisfying.

It is known that sin had two consequences:

1. Angering God's heart by disobeying Him, rebellion against Him, and obeying the devil more than Him. The burnt offering referred to pleasing God and satisfying His justice.

2. The perdition of man and condemning him to death. The sin offering substituted him, in dying instead of him.

The whole burnt offering was a symbol of the Lord Christ, in pleasing the Father and offering an absolute obedience to Him. The sin offering was a symbol of the Lord Christ, in His death instead of us and satisfying the divine justice which ordains the death of the sinner. And this is what we learned from of old, which we still teach to others.

28. The whole burnt offering as a symbol for pleasing God

The whole burnt offering is the oldest sacrifice with which people drew near to God. Therefore, it was called oblation [that is, offering].[384] And we read that, after the ark landed on dry land, our father Noah "built an altar to the Lord, and took of every clean animal and of every clean bird, and offered burnt offerings on the altar. And the Lord smelled a soothing aroma. Then the Lord said in His heart, 'I will never again curse the ground for man's sake.'"[385]

And we note that the whole burnt offering was a reason for pleasing God and lifting His anger away. Also, it [consisted] of clean animals and birds. And the burnt offering continued, which is what the fathers offered before the Law of Moses. And of the offerings which God commanded Moses the prophet in Leviticus, the burnt offering was first in order, for pleasing God should be first. The burnt offering was called an offering[386] because through it they drew near[387] to God.

---

384 See Genesis 4:5.
385 Genesis 8:20–21.
386 See Leviticus 1:2.
387 The words "offering" and "draw near" are related in Arabic: *korban* and *takarab*, respectively.

29. The whole burnt offering was for pleasing [the Lord] and a sweet aroma to the Lord, and it was entirely offered to God, for the fire of divine justice

The Scripture says about the one offering it, "As acceptable before the Lord."[388] And it is said about this offering that it is "an offering made by fire, a sweet aroma to the LORD."[389] And this description is repeated three times in all its kinds.

The entire burnt offering was for the fire of divine justice, remaining in the fire, burning till it turns into ashes, without anyone eating of it. Neither the priest, nor the person offering it, nor his friends, eat of it—it is completely for the fire.

And the following is said in the law of the burnt offering: "The burnt offering shall be on the hearth upon the altar all night until morning, and the fire of the altar shall be kept burning on it.... And the fire on the altar shall be kept burning on it; it shall not be put out. And the priest shall burn wood on it every morning.... A fire shall always be burning on the altar; it shall never go out."[390] It remains in the fire till it turns into ashes.[391]

30. The whole burnt offering is a symbol of the Lord Christ in satisfying the divine justice.

It is a symbol of pleasing[392] the Father in the work of redemption. The grain offering of flour was also a symbol for pleasing the Father, through His [i.e. the Son's] righteous life in His Incarnation before the crucifixion.[393] And so it was said about the grain offering also that it is "an offering made by fire, a sweet aroma to the LORD,"[394] and that it is "most holy."[395]

---

388   Leviticus 1:3 LXX, OSB.
389   Leviticus 1:9, 13, 17.
390   Leviticus 6:8–13.
391   See Leviticus 6:10.
392   Or: satisfying.
393   See Leviticus 2.
394   Leviticus 2:2, 9, 12.
395   Leviticus 2:3, 10.

The whole burnt offering and the grain offering of flour were a symbol of the Lord Christ, in His Incarnation and His accomplishing the work of redemption, each of which was "a sweet aroma to the Lord." Neither of them was a symbol for the forgiveness of man's sins. For this, the sin offering and trespass offering were symbols. The Passover sacrifice was also a symbol for man's salvation from perdition.

And the expression "a sweet aroma to the Lord" reminds us of the prophecy of Isaiah concerning the crucifixion of Christ, in which it was said regarding the Father that "It pleased the LORD to bruise Him."[396]

31. Pleasing God is a great virtue in the Scriptures.

With this the psalm begins, saying, "O Lord, You were pleased with Your land."[397] And concerning the sacrifices, it says, "Whatever man ... who offers his gifts in accord with any agreed-on offering or any offering of choice which they offer to God as a whole burnt offering—to be acceptable[398] on your behalf..."[399] On the life of virginity, the Apostle says, "He who is unmarried cares for the things of the Lord—how he may please the Lord."[400] And on the Liturgy and worship, he says, "Present your bodies a living sacrifice, holy, acceptable[401] to God, which is your reasonable service."[402] And concerning the pleasure of the Lord, the psalm says, "The LORD takes pleasure in those who fear Him,"[403] and the Scripture says, "When a man's ways please the LORD, He makes even his enemies to be at peace with him."[404]

To please the Lord, we find that the first four commandments

---

396 Isaiah 53:10.
397 Psalms 84:1 LXX, OSB.
398 In Arabic this word is the same as "pleasing."
399 Leviticus 22:18–19 LXX, OSB.
400 1 Corinthians 7:32.
401 In Arabic this word is the same as "pleasing."
402 Romans 12:1.
403 Psalms 147:11.
404 Proverbs 16:7.

of the ten commandments concern the Lord, before the commandments which concern the dealing with men. And likewise in the Lord's prayer we ask about what belongs to God first, before asking about what belongs to us. Of the beautiful things on pleasing God, we find the psalmist speaking to the angels in the psalm, saying, "Bless the LORD, all you His hosts, you ministers of His, who do His pleasure."[405] But how wonderful is the saying concerning pleasing the Father, which the Lord Christ said, "And He who sent Me is with Me. The Father has not left Me alone, for I always do those things that please Him."[406]

32. Speaking ill of appeasing God

Perhaps some might ask about the reason for mentioning all these quotes on pleasing God. It is because "the writer" sadly speaks ill of pleasing God, and so he says, "We find in the theory of redemption as appeasement of God, that the operation of redemption ends by the Son appeasing[407] the Father. And then the conversation is over, and the tragic novel ends by God recovering His honor."

It is not the recovery of honor, but the divine justice receiving its due.

And he says, "And the idea of appeasing God, though it is derived from the Old Testament, for 'Jehovah'—the consuming fire—in the Old Testament, became in the birth of the Son of God and the revelation of His sonship, a Father who pours His Spirit, instead of the curse, upon all men. Therefore, the image of God in this theory—and He seeks for someone to satisfy His justice and His honor—does not fit now with 'For God so loved the world that He gave His only begotten Son.'[408]"

We say that there is no disagreement between the Old and New Testaments, and no disagreement between Jehovah and the Father! And the expression "consuming fire" is present in the New

---

405 Psalms 103:21.
406 John 8:29.
407 Or: pleasing.
408 John 3:16.

Testament, where St. Paul the Apostle says, "For our God is a consuming fire."[409]

And our God, of whom he says that "a Father who pours His Spirit, instead of the curse," is the one who permitted that the Christ be a sin and a curse for our sakes. As St. Paul the Apostle says, "Christ has redeemed us from the curse of the law, having become a curse for us (for it is written, 'Cursed is everyone who hangs on a tree')."[410] And he says, "For He made Him who knew no sin to be sin for us, that we might become the righteousness of God in Him."[411]

And God of the New Testament, of whom it is said, "For God so loved the world," and "who pours His Spirit upon all men," is the one who permitted that Ananias and Sapphira die and die immediately because they lied to the Spirit of God.[412] God is the same in the New and Old Testaments, "with whom there is no variation or shadow of turning."[413] It is utterly uncalled-for to speak ill of Him, that "He seeks for someone to satisfy His justice and His honor." Or the writer's saying, "God the Father here is the one seeking to appease man who is wronged, rejected, humiliated, and persecuted, pursuing to bring him back to his first honor."

This last statement leads us to ask, "If man were wronged, then who wronged him?" Man is the one who wronged himself by his sin and lost his honor by his pride.

33. To whom was the price paid?

On the subject of redemption, the following question remains: To whom was the price paid?

The price which the Lord Christ paid is His death on the cross. This is so, because the Scripture says, "For the wages of sin is

---

409 Hebrews 12:29.
410 Galatians 3:13.
411 2 Corinthians 5:21.
412 See Acts 5:3–9.
413 James 1:17.

death."[414] And so He shed His pure, precious blood for our sakes.

And it is clear that the price was paid to the one to whom the right belongs, and that is divine justice. For divine justice was the one that demanded that the sinner dies; he who was subjected to God's judgment "shall surely die,"[415] and according to the Lord's saying through the mouth of Ezekiel the prophet, "The soul who sins shall die."[416]

So when Christ died instead of us, He offered His life to divine justice in place of man's life, so the divine justice received its due. But the writer says, "The blood which Christ offered [as] a price and ransom, He did not deliver it to anyone but us ... for we own the blood of Christ; we drink it, and yet without a price ... and It, as a price for our ransom, was added to our account." And he says that Christ "gave us His death that it may be our death. And He gave us His blood, which was shed, that it may be our blood ... For He did not die far from us, but died in our body, our blood, and our flesh. For we are partakers in this body and blood, and we still partake in It."

We would like to discuss this opinion.

34. Was the price of redemption paid to us?

The right does not belong to us, but on the contrary, we are debtors, whether we owe little or much. And the Lord Christ said concerning these two kinds, "And when they had nothing with which to repay, he freely forgave them both."[417] But we, as the Apostle said, "were dead in trespasses and sins."[418]

The price of redemption was offered to the divine justice. As for the Mystery of the Eucharist, It is not a price we are deserving of, but is a free gift which was granted to us, and not a price.

---

414 Romans 6:23.
415 Genesis 2:17.
416 Ezekiel 18:20.
417 Luke 7:42.
418 Ephesians 2:1.

And if the blood of Christ became our blood, as the writer says, so do we drink our own blood? And if Christ died in our flesh and blood, as he says, so did we share in paying the price? Or was the price paid to us? [This is] a strange matter, of which none of the Fathers have made mention!

After all this, we may ask, "What is the starting point [leading] to all the theological problems into which the writer fell?" It is his idea on intentional sin.

35. The writer sees that there was no sacrifice offered for the remission of intentional and purposeful sin.

He says, "There is no restitutive sacrifice whatsoever for intentional sin, which is deserving of death, in the entire law of the Old Testament. For all the sacrifices are for unintentional sins only."

He also says, "All the sin offerings which the Old Testament specified are, as we have previously repeatedly mentioned, only valid in case of unintentional sin … that is not intentional. As for intentional sins, which are purposeful and by one's will, there is no sacrifice for them at all in the entire law of Moses. And said in a clearer way, it is impossible to substitute or exchange life for life in case of intentional sin."

Also he says, "For here it is impossible for the sacrifice of Christ to be counted in place of the sinner, or on behalf of the sinner, or instead of the sinner. For the sin is intentional sin, and the sinner necessarily shall surely die, and it is impossible for any kind of sacrifice to be offered on his behalf!"

Again he says, "The sacrifice of Christ is death of the sinner in actuality! Christ took a body which is in its truth the body of man as a whole, the body of all sinners… It is the selfsame body of every sinner."

And this idea led to all the previous points we have discussed. Therefore, we should discuss his idea on intentional sin.

36. This thought causes confusion and despair.

Remission of sin in the Old Testament was connected with offering a sacrifice, and "Without shedding of blood there is no remission."[419] Therefore, if there were not a sacrifice offered for intentional sin, while most sins which people commit are intentional, how would people feel if they saw that their sins are not remitted, and they live and die without having their sins remitted? Would not this thought cause people to fall into despair and their minds to become confused?

And what would they say about God and about the verses related to the remission of sins? And what about the saying of the psalm, "Blessed is he whose transgression is forgiven, whose sin is covered. Blessed is the man to whom the LORD does not impute iniquity."[420] And what about what the Lord said in the Book of Ezekiel the prophet about the person who repents, "He shall surely live; he shall not die. None of the transgressions which he has committed shall be remembered against him."[421] Or what the Lord said in the Book of Jeremiah the prophet, "For I will forgive their iniquity, and their sin I will remember no more."[422]

How can there be forgiveness? And how can there be remission, and there are no sacrifices and no shedding of blood?

37. The example of sacrifices on the great day of atonement

We will mention a clear example of sacrifices for intentional sins: sacrifices on the great day of atonement, whether the high priest offers them for himself or for the people's sins. On that day the high priest offers a bull for a sin offering, "and make atonement for himself and for his house."[423] Then he offers another sin offering, "So he shall make atonement for the Holy Place, because of the uncleanness of the children of Israel, and because of their

---

419 Hebrews 9:22.
420 Psalms 32:1–2.
421 Ezekiel 18:21–22.
422 Jeremiah 31:34.
423 Leviticus 16:11.

transgressions, for all their sins."⁴²⁴

So, were there in all these sins, transgressions, and uncleanness, of Aaron, his house, and all the children of Israel, no intentional sin? Were all these iniquities unintentional sins? This is impossible. Who would believe that the great day of atonement was only for unintentional sins? I wonder at the audacity with which it is said, "For intentional sin, which is deserving of death, there is no substitutionary sacrifice in the entire law of Moses."

38. Other examples on sacrifices for forgiveness

Here we find that Nehemiah, in reforming the condition after returning from captivity, spoke about "the sin offerings to make atonement for Israel."⁴²⁵ And it is known that they were intentional and on purpose, that they married foreign women, which made Ezra the priest weep, pluck out some of the hair of his head, and tear his garment.⁴²⁶

And St. Paul the Apostle in his epistle to the Hebrews says, "For every high priest taken from among men is appointed for men in things pertaining to God, that he may offer both gifts and sacrifices for sins.... Because of this he is required as for the people, so also for himself, to offer sacrifices for sins."⁴²⁷ So, is a high priest appointed to offer both gifts and sacrifices for unintentional sins only which the people have committed?

39. David the king's intentional sin

Committing the sin of adultery with Bathsheba the wife of Uriah the Hittite was undoubtedly an intentional sin, and also his attempt at covering up this sin through deception, then contriving to kill Uriah, and marrying his wife.⁴²⁸

---

424 Leviticus 16:16.
425 Nehemiah 10:33.
426 See Ezra 9:3.
427 Hebrews 5:1, 3.
428 2 Samuel 11.

So, did David the prophet die without his sins being remitted, in that there is no sacrifice for intentional sins, according to the opinion of the writer? No, [he did not die before the remission of his sins], for David the prophet praises the Lord for His forgiveness, and says, "Bless the LORD, O my soul; and all that is within me, bless His holy name! ... Who forgives all your iniquities."[429] And how did David know that all his iniquities—intentional—were forgiven? From what Nathan the prophet said to him, "The LORD also has put away your sin; you shall not die."[430]

40. Redemption does not mean the death of the sinner in actuality! But it is the death of Christ instead of him.

Finally, let us precisely learn what the meaning of redemption is. Redemption is not the death of the sinner in actuality! But it is the death of Christ instead of him. For the death of the sinner is a punishment and not redemption.

But redemption is the death of the Redeemer instead of him or in his place. The Lord Christ accomplished this on the cross, from His exceedingly great love for us. And He did not take the body of sinners and die through it, as the writer says, but died in His pure body which is alone without sin.

But the writer calls this doctrine of the Church, "Substitutionary theory," a mere theory which requires that he discusses it, and not a doctrine which all believe in. And he sees that this was used in the Old Testament, to [remit] unintentional sins only. As for the New Testament, it cannot be applied, but the sinner must die in actuality.

---

429 Psalms 103:1, 3.
430 2 Samuel 12:13.

CHAPTER NINE

On the Mystery of the Eucharist

1. The following questions bring us face-to-face with several dangerous matters, which are the following:

✤ The danger of being influenced by reading foreign books that are alien to our doctrine, especially those related to biblical criticism. Then this reading is turned to doctrine, and then the person spreads it.

✤ The danger that some Sunday school and youth servants study what they read without examination, even if it is against the doctrine of the Church and her Tradition!

✤ The danger of admiring any new understanding and adopting it, without respecting what we have received from the Fathers throughout many generations.

✤ The danger of sowing doubt into people concerning what we have received of familiar and inherited teachings.

Therefore, I saw that it is necessary to address these issues and such like them, and explain them to our children, out of my responsibility to preserve the teaching of the Church pure from any blemish, that our generation may hand it down to the coming generations sound as it has been handed down to us.

As an example, regarding his book on the Eucharist, it is necessary that we address several points which the author mentioned, and we will explain them to the reader.

2. Attacking the statement "The seven Mysteries of the Church."

The author says, "The first one who specified these Mysteries of the Church to the number seven is the Roman Catholic Church by Peter Lombard, the Bishop of Paris, and others with him. Thomas Aquinas accepted it and made it a law in the Council of Florence in 1439. The Byzantine Church took this tradition from the Catholic Church."

He also says, "Then this tradition entered the Coptic Church, and the first mention of it we have access to is what appeared in the manuscript known by the name 'Purity of Souls.' And this is [attributed] to an unknown priest… and is thought not to be Coptic Orthodox."

And he says, "And anyway, we have not found any mention of the specification of the Mysteries of the Church to the number seven in the manuscript of the scholar Ibn Kabr, known by the name 'The Lamp of Darkness in Explaining the Service.' And he is the most important and meticulous of those who wrote on the Mysteries in the last centuries. And he did not even mention them together, but they appear fewer than seven in his writings, and were scattered throughout the book…"

Then the author mentions the mystery of the Trinity, the mystery of the Divinity, the mystery of the Incarnation and redemption, the mystery of the gospel,[431] the mystery of the kingdom of God,[432] the mystery of the faith,[433] the mystery of godliness,[434] and other mysteries.

3. The same matter is repeated in another of the author's books.

He says, "There are in the Church many other mysteries, not

---

431 Ephesians 6:19.
432 Mark 4:11.
433 1 Timothy 3:9.
434 1 Timothy 3:16.

counted as part of the seven Mysteries... for example, during the consecration of monks, the Holy Spirit descends through prayer and works by His grace in the consecrated person, for the preservation of his chastity and death to the lusts of the world. And in the consecration of churches, the Holy Spirit descends through the prayer of the Bishop, to sanctify this place and devote it for prayer... and in the prayer of the dead, the Holy Spirit descends to receive His own temple," and he comments on this point, by saying, "When the priest prays, he asks and says 'from this soul,' indicating the presence of the soul during the prayer."

4. The diverse meanings of the word "mystery," and distinguishing the Mysteries of the Church from the uses of the word "mystery" in other places.

The word "mystery"[435] can harbor the meaning of "secret," or "sacrament," or "mystery."

The word "mystery" as an indication of an intellectual, theological, or historical concept: As the Apostle says, "Great is the mystery of godliness: God was manifested in the flesh."[436] Here the mystery of the Incarnation is a theological [concept]. Or his saying, "For I do not desire, brethren, that you should be ignorant of this mystery, lest you should be wise in your own opinion, that blindness in part has happened to Israel until the fullness of the Gentiles has come in."[437] Or his saying, "Behold, I tell you a mystery: We shall not all sleep, but we shall all be changed— in a moment, in the twinkling of an eye, at the last trumpet. For the trumpet will sound, and the dead will be raised incorruptible, and we shall be changed."[438] Here [it means] a revelation of what is going to happen in the future—a revelation or a prophecy.

As for the seven Mysteries of the Church, they are something

---

435 In Arabic there is a single word for the English "secret," "sacrament," and "mystery."
436 1 Timothy 3:16.
437 Romans 11:25.
438 1 Corinthians 15:51–52.

other than all these matters which concern knowledge. So, what are they?

5. What are the Mysteries of the Church?

The Mystery of the Church is an invisible grace which God grants through a visible rite (prayer or sometimes a substance).

For example, in the Mystery of Baptism, the invisible grace is the new birth of water and the Spirit,[439] and regeneration, and the death of the old man.[440] All this is through a visible work, that is, the immersion into the water of Baptism.

And the Mystery of Myron (the Holy Anointing) is an invisible grace and the indwelling of the Spirit in man[441] or the sanctification of things, through a manifest work or the anointing with the Holy Myron. And in the past, at the beginning of the apostolic era, this was done through the laying on of the apostles' hands.[442]

And the Mystery of Repentance is an invisible grace through Confession and the absolution of the priest.

And the Mystery of the Priesthood is an invisible grace, an authority to practice the Mysteries, and an authority to remit sins or retain them[443]. And this Mystery is done through the laying on of the hand and the blowing of the Holy Spirit.

And so, the rest of the Mysteries of the Church are all invisible graces.

6. Confusing people's minds is not permitted, nor sowing doubt in what has been handed down to them, through speaking about the word "mystery" which signifies knowledge.

---

439 See John 3:5.
440 See Romans 6.
441 See 1 Corinthians 3:16.
442 See Acts 8 and 19.
443 John 20:22–23.

An example is what is said about "the mystery, which from the beginning of the ages has been hidden,"[444] or the mystery of the gospel "according to the revelation of the mystery kept secret since the world began,"[445] or "the mystery of godliness: God was manifested in the flesh,"[446] that is, the mystery of the Incarnation.

We have been entrusted with the matters that concern people's faith, and we are not permitted to confuse people's minds within the Church; sufficient is what they encounter of sowing of doubt through other denominations outside the Church.

The consecration of churches is not a new Mystery to be added to the seven Mysteries of the Church, according to the author, for it is part of the Mystery of Holy Myron.

And the consecration of monks is not a Mystery of the Church. Rather, it is the funeral prayer that is prayed on them, considering that they have died to the world, [and is accompanied] by advice and readings.

And the prayer over the dead is not a mystery, for it is merely an intercessional prayer, asking for their intercessions, in which the Holy Spirit does no come to receive His temple. And the soul is not present during the prayer, for as soon as the soul departs [from the body], it goes to the place of waiting, as the Lord said to the right-hand thief, "Today you will be with Me in Paradise."[447] And we mention the souls of the dead in every commemoration of the departed, without their being present with us.

7. The washing of the feet of the disciples before Communion.

Another point mentioned in his book on the Eucharist is the washing of the feet of the disciples before Communion.[448] It is known that the washing of their feet symbolizes the purity which

---

444 Ephesians 3:9.
445 Romans 16:25.
446 1 Timothy 3:16.
447 Luke 23:43.
448 See John 13.

was necessary for them before Communion. Therefore, after He washed their feet, the Lord said, "'He who is bathed needs only to wash his feet, but is completely clean; and you are clean, but not all of you.' For He knew who would betray Him."[449]

The washing of the disciples' feet was also a lesson on humility, and therefore the Lord said to them, "If I then, your Lord and Teacher, have washed your feet, you also ought to wash one another's feet."[450]

But the author considers that the Lord's washing of His disciples' feet was a mystical fellowship in the death with Him. And he points to the alabaster flask of fragrant oil which Mary poured and with which she anointed the feet of Christ, so the Lord said, "She has kept this for the day of My burial."[451]

So the author says that by washing the feet of the disciples, He was preparing them to die with Him, and that the washing of the feet was equivalent to the burial[452] of the whole body; and that "Christ saw in that a work equivalent to the burial of the whole body," "and so, the washing of the disciples' feet with the divine hands was a purifying work equivalent to the burial of the whole body, and as though He had beforehand shrouded them by washing their feet with His hands," "that is, Christ desired to make from the washing of the disciples' feet a mystical fellowship in the death with Him, a death leading to resurrection, glory and one portion in the prepared kingdom."

8. Everything the author said concerning this, does not agree with the biblical understanding of the necessity of purity before Communion and of giving them a lesson on humility.

As for their fellowship in the death with Him, it came later, for most of the apostles were martyred for the sake of His name. As for

---

449 John 13:10–11.
450 John 13:14.
451 John 12:7.
452 Literally: shrouding. This is the same word used in the verse above.

the death with the Lord with respect to the rest of the believers, this takes place in Baptism, according to the saying of the Apostle, "Or do you not know that as many of us as were baptized into Christ Jesus were baptized into His death? Therefore, we were buried with Him through baptism,"[453] and his saying also, "[You were] buried with Him in baptism."[454]

With respect to the Mystery of the Eucharist, instead of washing the feet, the priest washes his hands before Liturgy while saying, "I will wash my hands in innocence; so I will go about Your altar, O LORD,"[455] and he says to the Lord also, "Purge me with hyssop, and I shall be clean; wash me, and I shall be whiter than snow."[456] All these matters are a symbol of purity before Communion, and have nothing to do with burial[457] and the shrouding of the whole body.

The Lord Christ said concerning Mary, "She has kept this for the day of My burial," because that was at the beginning of Passion Week, "six days before the Passover."[458] And it is unimaginable that He meant to prepare the disciples for burial[459] tens of years before their martyrdom. Linking between the washing of the disciples' feet and Mary's pouring of oil of spikenard is not acceptable, and it takes the reader away from the preparation, in purity, for the Mystery of the Eucharist.

9. Did Judas take Communion, and then the devil entered him?

The author says that Judas took Communion, then the devil entered him, for he says, "Judas lived in peace, hiding behind the darkness of his deeds, his hypocrisy, and his betrayals all [these] days. And he ate and drank with the disciples and the Lord, without any hindrance or harm, except at the hour of the revelation of the mystery of the

---

453 Romans 6:3–4.
454 Colossians 2:12.
455 Psalms 26:6.
456 Psalms 51:7.
457 Or: shrouding.
458 John 12:1.
459 Or: shrouding.

sacrificed love in the supper of the Eucharist. For when the piece of bread went into his belly, grace, power, and protection went out [of him]. And the Spirit whom he received from the Lord was taken away from him, so the devil entered him, and his understanding was blinded, and the whole world was darkened before him, to the point that he hanged himself."

We would like to say that the piece of bread which Judas took was not the Mystery of the Eucharist. When the Lord Jesus was asked about the person who would betray him, He said, "He who dipped his hand with Me in the dish will betray Me."[460] This is the narrative of Matthew the Evangelist, which resembles the narrative of Mark the Evangelist: "He answered and said to them, 'It is one of the twelve, who dips with Me in the dish.'"[461] And the phrase, "who dips with Me in the dish," does not at all indicate Communion wherein the Lord says, "Take, eat; this is My body.... Drink from it, all of you. For this is My blood"[462]

As for the phrase "piece of bread," it appeared in the Gospel of John, where, in response to their question, "'Lord, who is it?' Jesus answered, 'It is he to whom I shall give a piece of bread when I have dipped it.' And having dipped the bread, He gave it to Judas Iscariot, the son of Simon. Now after the piece of bread, Satan entered him.... Having received the piece of bread, he then went out immediately. And it was night."[463] The word "dip" occurs twice and does not signify His giving him Communion. As for Communion, the Gospel expressed It by "[He] broke it, and gave it."[464] And nearly the same expression appears in the first epistle to the Corinthians, "The Lord Jesus ... took bread; and when He had given thanks, He broke it and said, 'Take, eat; this is My body which is broken for you.'"[465] And likewise in the Communion of the cup, He "gave it to them, saying, 'Drink from it,'"[466] and *not*

---

460 Matthew 26:23.
461 Mark 14:20.
462 Matthew 26:26–27.
463 John 13:25–26, 30.
464 Matthew 26:26; Mark 14:22; Luke 22:19.
465 1 Corinthians 11:23–24.
466 Matthew 26:27.

dipping a piece of bread.

But the phrases "dipped the bread" or "a piece of bread when I have dipped it" indicate the eating of the Passover lamb, and not the eating of the Mystery of the Eucharist.

[See the introduction of the lectionary of Covenant Thursday].

In the evening of Covenant Thursday, there were the Passover supper, the Lord's Supper (the Mystery of the Eucharist), and praises between the two suppers. Judas attended the Passover supper and took the piece of bread, and the devil entered him. He then went out immediately. And it was night. And he did not attend the Mystery of the Eucharist.

And the Passover supper was not an ordinary supper but was a symbol of the sacrifice of Christ[467]. For when Judas took the symbol unworthily, he was not permitted to partake of that which it [the piece of bread] was a symbol of—the Body and Blood. So, he went out. Then the Lord offered this great Mystery to the eleven [disciples].

"He who has ears to hear, let him hear!"[468]

It was unimaginable that the Lord would offer His body and blood to Judas, while He declared that "it would have been good for that man if he had not been born."[469] So how would He give him the Promises, of which He had said before that "He who eats My flesh and drinks My blood abides in Me, and I in him,"[470] and, "Whoever eats My flesh and drinks My blood has eternal life, and I will raise him up at the last day"[471]? How does He give him Communion and give him an opportunity to "be guilty of the

---

467 See 1 Corinthians 5:7.
468 Matthew 13:43.
469 Matthew 26:24.
470 John 6:56.
471 John 6:54.

body and blood of the Lord,"[472] "not discerning the Lord's body,"[473] according to the Apostle? How does He give him Communion, while He declared, at [the time of] the washing of the feet, that he was not clean? For He said to the disciples, "'You are clean, but not all of you.' For He knew who would betray Him."[474] And if the devil entered Judas by his merely taking a piece of bread from the Passover supper, how would he take the body of the Lord in the Mystery of the Eucharist after the devil had [already] entered him? It suffices that he took part in the Passover celebration.

10. The author also denies that the Lord Christ ate the Passover with His disciples on Covenant Thursday.

In one of his books he tries to prove that the Master Lord did not eat the Passover with His disciples, but the Supper of the Lord was one entire day before the Passover, and by that he goes against our liturgical books, the readings of the Holy Pascha Week, and the account of the Gospels! It is related in the Gospel of Matthew:

> Now on the first day of the Feast of the Unleavened Bread the disciples came to Jesus, saying to Him, "Where do You want us to prepare for You to eat the Passover?" And He said, "Go into the city to a certain man, and say to him, 'The Teacher says, "My time is at hand; I will keep the Passover at your house with My disciples."'" So the disciples did as Jesus had directed them; and they prepared the Passover.[475]

So, is it plausible that the Lord says, "I will keep the Passover at your house with My disciples," then sends His disciples to prepare the Passover, and after all that He does not keep the Passover with His disciples? And in the Gospel of St. Mark, nearly the same words are said:

---

472   1 Corinthians 11:27.
473   1 Corinthians 11:29.
474   John 13:10–11.
475   Matthew 26:17–19.

Now on the first day of Unleavened Bread, when they killed the Passover lamb, His disciples said to Him, "Where do You want us to go and prepare, that You may eat the Passover?" ... [He said to them], "Say to the master of the house, 'The Teacher says, "Where is the guest room in which I may eat the Passover with My disciples?"'" ... And they prepared the Passover.[476]

The same thing is recounted in the Gospel of Luke.[477]

The author acknowledges these accounts of the Gospels, saying, "The reader might understand from these readings that Christ ate the Passover with His disciples, and this was the Lord's Supper in which He established the Mystery of the Eucharist, according to the words or literal utterance of the account of the three Gospels, but..."

But here comes in the school of biblical criticism.

11. Did Christ slaughter Himself, by intention, on Covenant Thursday?

In one of his books the writer says, "When Christ slaughtered Himself by intention and delivered His body to His disciples to eat in the Mystery of the Eucharist, He revealed Himself that He is the true, new Passover." And he also said, "The Lord, in these moments, was slaughtering Himself by intention and prophecy."

We would like to stop here at the statement "He slaughtered Himself" and examine its theological, historical, and biblical meaning. Did the Lord Christ slaughter Himself, or did the Jews slaughter Him? Of Him St. Peter said to the Jews, "[You] killed the Prince of life."[478] And he said concerning the healing of the lame man at the Beautiful Gate, "Let it be known to you all ... that by the name of Jesus Christ of Nazareth, whom you crucified ... by

---

476 Mark 14:12–16.
477 See Luke 22:7–8.
478 Acts 3:15.

Him this man stands here before you whole."[479] The expression "slaughtered Himself" is not acceptable theologically nor biblically. It can be said that the Lord Christ offered Himself to be slaughtered, or offered Himself to be put to death, but we cannot say that He slaughtered Himself or put Himself to death. Rather He accepted death from [the hand of] another.

12. The writer has written the opposite of the phrase "Christ slaughtered Himself by intention and prophecy" in two of his other books.

In one of his books, he says, "Christ, in the supper on Thursday, did not explain theoretically how he would be slaughtered on Friday, but went ahead of the events. One whole day before the cross, He offered Himself slaughtered to His disciples, not as a mere work of the works of intention and demonstration, but as an actual act of breaking, slaughtering, and shedding [of blood], more actual, deeper, and clearer than that which happened on Friday on the cross."

And in another book, he says, "He was not prophesying here about what would happen to Him on the cross, of the shedding of His blood ... but now He brought forth to them the event in all its details from the depth of eternity—and not time—even passing over the future. And He gave the selfsame blood which He was about to pour on the cross, that they may drink of it." And he adds, "He gave them the mystery of His death, the mystery of His blood, the mystery of His resurrection, and the mystery of His life, altogether in the broken bread and mixed wine, that He may dwell in their depths, their being, and their innermost parts, as a true death and true resurrection, for eternal life..." and he adds also, "As an act of redemption effective through His power. And this is above time, before time, and after time. He remits the sins of the past, present, and future, 'which is shed for many for the remission of sins,'[480] and eternal life."

---

479 Acts 4:10.
480 Matthew 26:28.

Was the redemption accomplished on Thursday? And were the sins of the past, present, and future remitted on Thursday?

And concerning what happened on Thursday too, he says in one of his books, "Not as a broken bread or mixed wine anymore, but a 'slaughtered body' actually, before them as a true, divine Passover. For the death of the cross, on Friday, is not merely an offering to the Father for the sins of the world only, but a sacrifice of love and continual supper of which the whole world eats."

So, was the redemption accomplished on Thursday, and on Friday He added the sacrifice of love?

In the same book, the fulfillment of propitiation is linked to the condition of actual participation in it, and he says, "A personal sacrifice of love, in which propitiation is not fulfilled, except through the actual sharing in it…" And he also says, "As a sacrifice for salvation and remission of sins, the actual eating of the body and drinking of the blood must accomplish it, according to the mystery which He fulfilled in the Thursday supper. And by that only, the propitiation is fulfilled, and remission is fulfilled, and the union with Christ is fulfilled, for the continuation in eternal life."

13. Here the reader is perplexed: Did the redemption and the shedding of the blood of Christ take place on Thursday or on Friday?

Was the shedding of the blood of Christ on Thursday, without suffering, crucifixion, and [the crown of] thorns? And was His blood shed twice, on Thursday and Friday?

The writer makes the reader more perplexed, saying concerning Thursday, "He commanded them to eat of It and drink, not as a broken bread or mixed wine anymore, but a 'slaughtered body' actually, explaining by this that the mystery of Friday is present before them as a true, divine Passover. For the death of the cross, on Friday, is not merely an offering to the Father for the sins of the world only, but a sacrifice of love and continual supper of which the whole world eats." Then he says, "A personal sacrifice of love, in which propitiation is not fulfilled, except through the actual sharing in it… And by that only, the propitiation is fulfilled, and remission is fulfilled."

What about then our Agpeya prayers in the sixth hour, where we say, "O You, who on the sixth day and in the sixth hour were nailed to the cross, for the sin which our father Adam dared to commit in Paradise," and we also say to Him, "[O You] who were nailed to the cross in the sixth hour, and killed sin by the tree, and by Your death You made alive the dead man, whom You created with Your own hands, and had died in sin." Do we, after all this, say that propitiation was not fulfilled on the cross, but is fulfilled in Communion? And what is the meaning of our saying to Him, "You wrought salvation in the midst of all the earth, O Christ our God, as You stretched Your holy hands on the cross"? So, was that which was fulfilled on Covenant Thursday for the remission of sins, and that which was fulfilled on Friday a sacrifice of love and a continual supper?

The depth of the love of the Lord for us was [made manifest] in His death on the cross, in which He bore our sins and He remitted them for us and erased them by His blood. Why [do you] then confuse the people's minds?

14. Did the Father neither seek nor ask that Christ sheds His blood?

Then what is the Father's position toward the sacrifice of the Son on the cross? Did the Father neither seek nor ask that Christ sheds His blood?

The writer says in an article he wrote and published in the Journal of Mark, October 2003, "The blood of Christ was shed. And the saintly fathers confirm that the Father did not seek nor ask that Christ sheds His blood. And this negates the claim that the death of Christ was a divine requirement by the Father [as] satisfaction of the divine justice."

And of course, these words are absolutely not in agreement

with the Holy Scriptures, in which it is said, "For God so loved the world that He gave His only begotten Son, that whoever believes in Him should not perish but have everlasting life."[481] So, how is it said that the Father did not seek nor ask that Christ sheds His blood, while the Father is the one who gave His Son for the salvation of the world? As it is also said, "In this the love of God was manifested toward us, that God has sent His only begotten Son into the world, that we might live through Him. In this is love, not that we loved God, but that He loved us and sent His Son to be the propitiation for our sins."[482]

So, how can "the Father has sent His Son to be the propitiation for our sins, that we might live through Him" be reconciled with "the Father did not seek nor ask that Christ sheds His blood"? And how is it that the Father did not seek nor ask, while it was written about the Lord Christ that He "became obedient to the point of death, even the death of the cross."[483] Whom did He obey? Is it not the Father who gave Him up?

Also, how is it said, "that the shedding of the blood of Christ was not to the pleasure of the Father's heart"? While it is said of Him in the Book of Isaiah the prophet, "Yet it pleased the LORD to bruise Him; He has put Him to grief,"[484] Do we deny the Holy Scriptures, that we might believe contrary ideas? And he who has ears to hear, let him hear.

15. Were they accustomed to partaking of Communion after an agape supper feast?

The writer says in one of his books, "We do not forget the text which Paul the Apostle wrote, 'In the same manner He also took the cup after supper,'[485] which elucidates that the completion of the Mystery of the Eucharist—that is, the thanksgiving [prayer] on the

---

481 John 3:16.
482 1 John 4:9–10.
483 Philippians 2:8.
484 Isaiah 53:10.
485 1 Corinthians 11:25.

cup—came after finishing an agape feast." And he also says:

> And in this supper, and through it, "the mystery of divine thanksgiving" took place. That is, beside an ordinary supper and through it the Lord sanctified, by His hands and words, a single [piece of] bread of the bread placed [before Him] and a cup of wine at the beginning of the supper, and the wine at the end of the supper, where the bread becomes mystically His body, and all the disciples ate from It. Then they finished eating from all kinds of food. And after eating from these [kinds of] food, the Lord arose and washed the disciples' feet. And He sat again at the table and took a cup, which is called "the cup of blessing" or "the cup of thanksgiving," and prayed on it the thanksgiving prayer, that is the prayer of the Eucharist, and tasted and gave to the disciples. So they all drank from it… then they sang hymns for a long time and went out.

These are strange words, found only in foreign books, which the author relied on. And in them also is Communion after an ordinary supper and separation between partaking of the bread and wine.

16. Was there about an hour between the sanctification of bread and wine?

And in this hour they had [an ordinary] supper? The author says in one of his books:

> The Church received from the Apostles the rite of the Supper of the Lord, complete as a love feast (agape), which begins and ends with the Holy Mystery (the Eucharist). That is, it begins with the mystery of the breaking of bread and ends with the mystery of the cup of blessing. And in between there is an ordinary meal of all kinds of food and drinks, in which all those present partake.

And he also says:

All churches had made a special prayer rite for the agape and another rite for the Eucharist, except in Egypt where the agape feast remained connected with the Eucharist till the fifth century… and the Eucharist was offered in the evening.

These words contradict all three of our Divine Liturgies and the Church's rite of fasting in preparation for the Divine Liturgy and Communion. These words sow confusion into people's minds, as though fasting before Communion is not attributed to an apostolic decree[486].

17. Our analysis of the aforementioned.

We would say that St. Paul the Apostle, by mentioning "after supper,"[487] does not mean at all what this writer said, that it is "an ordinary supper" or "supper of all kinds of food." Rather, he mentioned this after the partaking of the Holy Body.

We note that in our Divine Liturgies the sanctification of the bread and wine is at the same time, with no interruption nor supper in between. What was published in his book is nothing but a sowing of confusion into people's minds and belittlement of the special rites of this Mystery which they have received. And it is unimaginable that people would partake of the Holy Mystery after having had an ordinary supper and after all kinds of food.

As for the agape [meal] of which the author spoke, it is the food they eat together after Communion, considering that they had been fasting for a long time. And it is impossible that this agape "of all kinds of food" contain the Mystery of Holy Communion. This is the result of reading foreign books which justify people's receiving Communion, in the West, without fasting or spiritual preparation.

---

486 Literally: handing down.
487 1 Corinthians 11:25.

18–19. Were they accustomed to receiving the Body in their hands? And were they accustomed to sometimes taking It to their homes?

The following was said in one of the writer's books:

> And in explaining the lawfulness of taking the blessing bread out of the church, to deliver it to the homes of the sick and those were absent out of necessity, we find that some rules prohibit it, while others do not prohibit it. But this confusion arises from [the fact] that the Eucharist Itself was taken by the believers to their homes. And this is when the rite for distribution of the Eucharist used to facilitate that. For each one of the communicants would be given a part of the Body in their hands, and they, by their free will, place It in their mouths. From here, believers would keep part of the Body in their hands and take It to their homes. But when the Church forbade this practice with strict canons—which we will address in the section on the Eucharist—it came in the course of these canons that it is forbidden to take the eulogia outside the church. By eulogia is meant the Eucharist Itself, for there was no difference in the word and its meaning back then.

We do not desire to address now the subject of the blessing bread, but we will stop at the statement "the Eucharist Itself was taken by the believers to their homes," and "For each one of the communicants would be given a part of the Body in their hands, and they, of their freedom, place It in their mouths." This matter applies to Westerners, who do not give the Body into the communicants' mouths, but in their hand. But that this is mentioned as part of Orthodox history, calls for wonder and sows doubt and confusion. Also it appears to be a justification of Westerners' way of partaking of Communion.

The priest washes his hands thoroughly, lest some pearls of the Body cling to them, and he drinks that water with extreme care. But what about the communicants who take the Body in their hand, and by their free will place It in their mouths? How many pearls of the Body cling to their hand or fingers and they overlook Them? As for taking the Body to the communicants' homes, this matter is even stranger. And we do not believe that this has been mentioned in any historical reference, trustworthy for its Orthodoxy. As for what he wrote concerning the strict canons which forbade that, the writer mentioned "that it is forbidden to take the eulogia outside the church," the reader's understanding of the eulogia is the [blessed] bread distributed for blessing.

Also the Eucharist is not the Body only, but this Mystery includes the Blood also. So, how is the whole Eucharist taken to [the believers'] homes? Or do communicants take the Body in hand and might carry It home? And what about the Blood in this whole story? This sows confusion, undoubtedly. And this confusion either leads to doubt in the ancient Apostolic handing-down, or in that the rite which is currently followed [suggesting that it] does not have ancient, patristic roots. Each of these matters has its dangers.

20. Did deacons distribute the Body and Blood?

The following was said in one of the writer's books:

> From the Eucharist of Justin Martyr, it is made clear that deacons were entrusted with presenting the Eucharist, parts of the Eucharist, the Body and Blood to each of the believers in his place, but they would even keep parts of the Eucharist also for those who were absent.

The problem of the specialization of deacons must be researched well in history. In the past, the word deacon referred to a full deacon completely devoted to service, who would grow his beard and wear a garment similar to that of priests. If deacons distributed the Eucharist in the past, what was the priest's role in the distribution? Did the priests pray the Liturgy, while the deacons distributed the Body and Blood?

What is the meaning also of the Mysteries were given to each one in his place? Do people themselves come for Communion, or do the Body and Blood go to where the people are? And what is the meaning of "keep parts of the Eucharist also for those who were absent"? The only exception the Church permits is giving Communion to the ill who are bedridden, and the priest performs this with an extremely meticulous procedure. As for the statement "distributing the Mysteries," it does not mean carrying Them to where the believers are standing, but it means that the Eucharist is given to the congregation also. But it is not fitting of the honor of the Holy Mystery that the deacon would walk with It to the believers.

21. Was the rite of the Offering of the Lamb a full Liturgy?

The writer says in one of his books, "Worshipping the items of the Eucharist while they are still bread and wine, before the sanctification, was a great stumbling block for Latin and Greek scholars ... to the point that some critics said that it was idol-worshipping."

Then he said:

The solution to this dilemma which mystified the scholars lies in a truth that is important and serious to the uttermost. That is, there is a whole, eucharistic, liturgical rite which all the churches of the East have ignored, and nothing is left of it except hints in passing. As for the churches of the West, they have completely dropped it. And this rite has not remained in its complete, detailed form except in Egypt. It is the rite called the Offering of the Lamb. And in its truth and according to the meaning which bears its name, it is the oldest sacramental rite in full, in which the bread and wine are offered to be sanctified, that they may become a lamb prepared for the burnt offering, or prepared at the beginning of Liturgy, to be offered to the Father as a rational Sacrifice and the bloodless service!

And in the same book he says, "It has become clear to us that the Offering of the Lamb rite is itself the Supper of the Lord rite, and it is a complete Liturgy by itself. It was included in the Liturgy of St. Basil, to preserve it from loss." And he also says, "From this it is clear that the bread and wine are not any longer—and we are here at the beginning—bread and wine, but are the King of kings and Lord of lords who has come to be sacrificed and to be given as food for the believers. And It is the pure Body which descended from the cross."

22. It is known that the sanctification of the Eucharist is accomplished by the descent of the Holy Spirit.

This is where the priest prays, saying, "That Your Holy Spirit may descend upon us and upon these gifts set forth, and purify them, change them, and manifest them as a sanctification of Your saints,"[488] "And this bread He makes into His holy Body,"[489] "And this cup also, the precious Blood of His New Covenant,"[490] and the people say, "Amen." Then after the litanies, the priest says, "The Holy Body … and the precious Blood,"[491] and the people worship.

After this the priest does not turn his gaze away from the Sacrifice, and when he blesses the people with "Peace be with all," he does not turn to them; and when he signs the Body and Blood [with the sign of the cross], he does not sign Them with his hand, but he signs the Body with the Blood, and signs the Blood with the Body.

Where is all this from the priest's going down to the nave of the church after the Offering of the Lamb during the raising of incense of the Pauline Epistle and the Catholic Epistle, the Litany of the Gospel, the reading of the Gospel, and the sermon? If the Offering of the Lamb were a complete Liturgy, why would there be prayers after it, and what is the point of the Liturgy? And why do the believers not receive Communion immediately after the Offering

---

488 The Divine Liturgy According to St. Basil – The Epiclesis.
489 The Divine Liturgy According to St. Basil – After the Epiclesis.
490 Ibid.
491 The Divine Liturgy According to St. Basil – Introduction to the Fraction.

of the Lamb? And if the sanctification occurred during the Offering of the Lamb, then the catechumens would be in attendance, and according to the rite of the early Church, they were not permitted to do so, for only the believers attended the Liturgy of the Faithful, after the sermon and the dismissal of the catechumens.

What occurs in the Offering of the Lamb is merely the blessing of them [i.e. the bread and wine], and not their sanctification, nor their turning [or changing] into the Body and Blood.

23. Is the Lord's Body here Christ and the Church?

The writer speaks in his book, taking as testimony the saying of St. Paul the Apostle concerning the partaking of the Body and Blood unworthily, that "he who eats and drinks in an unworthy manner eats and drinks judgment to himself, not discerning the Lord's body,"[492] and he says immediately after this, "The Body of the Lord here is Christ first, then the Church also, considering that she is His mystical body." So, do the believers partake [i.e. receive Communion] of the Church too?

What is this confusion between the Body of Christ in the Mystery of the Eucharist and the Church, considering that she is—spiritually—the body of Christ? And this has appeared also in some of his other books. The Body in the Mystery of the Eucharist is the Body that was born from the Virgin St. Mary. The Church, being the congregation of the believers, was not born from St. Mary, except in the book by the same author.

The Body of Christ in the Mystery of the Eucharist is a perfect Body, while the members of the Church are not yet completed, but we are waiting for new members who will be born and baptized, and others of the unbelievers who will join the faith. And there are many other differences which we will address in the next article on the Body of Christ, to make such matters clear.

24. Do we eat the Divine nature in the Eucharist?

---

492 1 Corinthians 11:29.

These words are said by the author in an audio recording of him about the Eucharist. And the same words appeared in one of his books: "We drink the Divinity—of course, mystically—and we drink the life-giving Blood, according to grace and not according to a bodily standard."

Of course, the Divinity is not eaten nor drunk. And the expressions, "We eat the Divine nature," and "We drink the Divinity," are absolutely not acceptable. And this is strange to the ear and understanding. "God is Spirit"[493] and it is not imaginable that we say, "We eat the Spirit," or, "We drink the Spirit." And the Lord Christ said, "Whoever eats My flesh and drinks My blood,"[494] and did not say, "Whoever eats My Divinity and drinks My Divinity."

25. What is the meaning of his saying, "The source from which Mark drew the information"?

He says in one of his books, "We have found from the aforementioned that the source from which Mark the Apostle drew his information, although it is not the same source from which each of Paul the Apostle and Luke the Evangelist drew their information…" And he also says, "Mark the Apostle goes deeper than Luke the Evangelist, because he has obtained a text that contains the terms that were said during the supper." In reality these statements take us away from the belief in the divine inspiration of the writing of the Gospels and the work of the Holy Spirit in this matter.

Regarding St. Paul the Apostle, his source on the Mystery of the Eucharist is clear: it is the Lord Christ Himself. For he says, "For I received from the Lord that which I also delivered to you: that the Lord Jesus on the same night in which He was betrayed took bread."[495] Concerning St. Mark, it is known that the Passover and the Lord's Supper were celebrated in his house in the upper room of Zion, and all the Apostles were present, and they knew and

---

493 John 4:24.
494 John 6:54.
495 1 Corinthians 11:23.

heard all that happened that night. It is meaningless then to speak about the source from which St. Mark drew his information.

Also how strange is his saying in one of his books, "Mark the Apostle used as reference in narrating some incidents, in which he did not participate, a source translated to him from Hebrew and Aramaic to Greek." It is known, however, that St. Mark knew Hebrew as he did Greek, and he was not at all in need of a translator. But even in the Roman Catholic [Church], it is said that Mark the Apostle used to translate for Peter the Apostle, according to *Les Saints d'Egypte by Cheneau.*[496]

26. Do the Priesthood and the Eucharist descend from eternity?

The writer says in one of his books:

> Ambrose, in his investigation of this Mystery, proves that the Mystery of the Eucharist which we now celebrate is older, concerning its historical date, than the era of the sacrifices from Moses! And this truth is worthy of consideration. For the Priesthood and the Eucharist descend originally from everlasting [*al'abadia*], from God, from beyond time and history. For Melchizedek is originally without beginning of days nor end of life.

We, of course, agree that Melchizedek was the priest of God Most High, and that he brought out bread and wine when he met Abraham the patriarch. This was before the time of Moses and the laws of its sacrifices. But this does not mean that the Priesthood and the Eucharist descend originally from beyond everlasting [*al'abadia*] and history. The author, of course, means "eternity"[497] [*al'azalia*] and not everlasting [*al'abadia*], for *al'azalia* means that

---

496   See P. Cheneau, Les Saints d'Egypte: lectures édifiantes, instructives, agréables 1. (Jerusalem: Couvent Des RR. PP. Franciscains, 1923), 497.
497   In Arabic the word *al'azalia* means "with no beginning," which is translated here to "eternity," though in English "eternity" means both with no beginning and no end; and the word *al'abadia* means "everlasting," i.e. with no end.

which has no beginning, while everlasting meaning that which has no end.

For that which is before history—or that which is in eternity [*al'azalia*]—had no need of priesthood, for who does the Priesthood serve before history, with care, teaching, and the Mysteries? And the Eucharist, which is given for us for salvation and remission of sins, for whom is It given before history?

As for what is said concerning Melchizedek that "without father, without mother, without genealogy, having neither beginning of days nor end of life, but made like the Son of God,"[498] this does not at all mean that he is eternal [*azali*], for no one is eternal but God alone. And this does not mean that he was one of the appearances of Christ in the Old Testament! Rather, he is "made like the Son of God" in the Priesthood, that is, Priesthood that is not by inheritance from father or mother. Melchizedek was without father and without mother in the Priesthood, and his history was not fully known. For he suddenly appeared in Genesis 14, without beginning of days related of him, and he also disappeared without knowing an end to his days. So did St. John Chrysostom say in his exegesis on the seventh chapter of the epistle to the Hebrews.[499]

As for the Priesthood, it undoubtedly has a history, linked to the sins of men and their remission, and linked to the spiritual guidance of men. And the sin of men has a history and is not in eternity and beyond history.

27. Is God not "an another" with respect to man?

The author says in one of his books, "A person ... after he speaks, remains as 'an another' with respect to us. But God, when He spoke, spoke so that by the word He may enter our life, and become as a Self in self..." And he says on the same page, "God here, after speaking with man, did not become an another with respect to man. Having become God to man means that He has

---

498 Hebrews 7:3.
499 See John Chrysostom *The Homilies of St. John Chrysostom on the Epistle to the Hebrews* (NPNF[1] 14:423–424).

become closer to man than everything, but has become as the soul of man and his self! And based on this law itself, God in the Holy Scriptures did not speak at all except to prove this truth, deepen it, and ensure its enforcement."

What does it mean that God becomes not an another? Does He Himself become man's self, or does man become a God? This occasion compels me to write an article on man's deification, to answer these ideas and others like it in the books of this same author.

28. Does Christ create from His flesh and bones the new man?

The author says in one of his books, "Christ, from His flesh and bones, creates the new spiritual man every day." He repeats the same words in another of his books. The statement "from His flesh and bones" compels us to write a new article, named "The Body of Christ and the Mystical Body."

CHAPTER TEN

The Body of Christ and the Mystical Body

Introduction

The phrases "the body of Christ" and "the mystical body of Christ" represent, in the writings of the author, numerous complications and contradictions, as it will be shown in the following pages, especially the thoughts that appeared in several of his books.

We are concerned about the theological meanings contained in these books and the like, leading us to discussing all these points and presenting them to the reader, to make the theological understanding clear. We place all this before the dear reader in defense of the true faith.

"He who has ears to hear, let him hear!"[500]

1. What does the phrase "the body of Christ" mean?

The phrase "the body of Christ" has three uses:

1. It means the body of Christ which was born of the Virgin St. Mary, which was crucified for us, was buried and rose, ascended into the heavens, and sat down at the right hand of the Father.

2. It means the Church, as it came in Ephesians 5, for the Church

---

500 Matthew 13:43.

is His body and He is the head.[501]

3. The third meaning is used in the Mystery of the Eucharist, as the Lord said, "Take, eat; this is My body,"[502] and as St. Paul the Apostle mentioned in 1 Corinthians 11:27, 29.

Nevertheless, some people combine these three uses in one meaning. And I have explained the error of combining or confusing [these uses], and have responded to it in the series *Years with People's Inquiries*, yet I am obliged to go back to the same subject, for it has taken another form.

2. The body of Christ, meaning the Church, the bride of Christ.

The Church is the congregation of the believers, and was called the body of Christ, as we have mentioned. The Church was also called His bride, as John the Baptist said concerning Christ and the Church, "He who has the bride is the bridegroom,"[503] and as St. Paul the Apostle said, "'For this reason a man shall leave his father and mother and be joined to his wife, and the two shall become one flesh.' This is a great mystery, but I speak concerning Christ and the church."[504]

From here came this term, that Christ is the Bridegroom, and the Church is the bride. And so we find that the author of the book speaks of a holy matrimony between Christ and the Church. But when did this union between Him and her take place?

3. When was the Church born united with Christ?

The author says in one of his books:

> And by this the origin of the marriage is revealed to us, which was fulfilled by His uniting first with our body in the Virgin, from whom He took His bride which is the

---

501   See Colossians 1:18, 24.
502   Matthew 26:26.
503   John 3:29.
504   Ephesians 5:31–32.

body. So He was born united with her with His Divinity. That is, the Church was born united with Christ the day Christ was born. And consequently, every one of us was born in Bethlehem, so it became the birthplace of the redeemed humanity.

And concerning the body of Christ here we ask, what is it? And how was it formed? It is known that the Lord Christ took His body from the Virgin Mary through the work of the Holy Spirit; therefore, we say in the Orthodox Creed concerning the Hypostasis of the Son, "[He] came down from heaven, was incarnate of the Holy Spirit and of the Virgin Mary, and became man."

So, what is the meaning of the statement of the author on Christ, "by His uniting first with our body in the Virgin, from whom He took His bride which is the body"?

4. Is Christ's humanity the Church? And did He unite with our body?

We are reminded of his same understanding: "He was crucified in our body, suffered in our body, rose in our body, and was buried in our body," as it appeared in one of his books, and here he says that He was born of the Virgin by His uniting with our body.

So, did Christ take His bride—that is the Church—of Virgin Mary? Isn't there confusion in this between the body of Christ born of the Virgin and His body meaning the Church, that is the congregation of the believers? Did His body unite with His Divinity? Or did the Church unite with His Divinity?

He also says concerning the Church in another of his books, "Considering that she is His body, which He took from us, sanctified it, redeemed it, and granted it to us with **all His Divine attributes**... to join His Divine attributes to her account," and he adds, "Therefore, we are not surprised when we hear that the Father has stored in the Church all the attributes of the Son and His inheritance."

What are all the Divine, eternal[505] attributes of the Son, which were granted to the Church? Is this a progression towards the deification of the Church?

5. Did the Church unite with the Divinity of Christ?

Was the Church in the womb of the Virgin before the Gospel was preached? And before Christ began His mission, of teaching and salvation? And before the Holy Spirit descended on the disciples on Pentecost?

The Divinity of the Lord Christ united with His humanity. Therefore, if His humanity were the Church, that is the congregation of the believers, His Divinity, in His union with the Church, has united with all the congregation of the believers, every individual of the believers becoming a humanity united with the Divinity, fully like Christ! And we, who were not in existence during the birth of the Lord Christ, did the Divinity unite with us, as members in the Church? How and when? And if there were people who will join the body of the Church afterwards, who are not yet born, has the Divinity united with these in the womb of the Virgin before they are born? Or, will the Divinity unite with them, as member in the Church, when they are born in the future?

The Divinity's union with the Church is contrary to the distinctiveness of the Lord Christ in this nature, the nature of the incarnate God. And with this aforementioned thought [or understanding], He is considered as one of these believers. And on this point, we are reminded of that which appeared in one of his books by the same author, which we will address later.

6. Was the Church born on the day Christ was born?

On the day Christ was born, there was no Church; there was no congregation of the believers. The matter remained so throughout the thirty years which the Lord Christ lived after His Incarnation, before starting His mission and preaching. So, how was the Church

---

505 *Azalia*, i.e. with no beginning.

then born on the day He was born? Was she born without faith, without redemption, without Mysteries, and without the Bible?

If the Virgin Mary was the believer at the time Christ was born[506] and she represents the Church, was the Virgin Mary born from the womb of the Virgin Mary? And if the Church then was the small congregation of the believers, who were mentioned in the story of Nativity, like Elizabeth, the Magi, the shepherds, and Joseph the carpenter—and they represent a small church—how was this church born from the womb of the Virgin Mary?

Were all the members of the Church born without a father like Christ, through the work of the Holy Spirit? Does Christ have millions of blood brothers? A matter the human mind is incapable of understanding, and theology does not accept, and not one of the saintly Fathers of the teachers of the Church has said.

7. How did Bethlehem become the birthplace of the redeemed humanity?

The start of the faith in Christianity was in Jerusalem[507] and not Bethlehem. Also, humanity was not redeemed on the day Christ was born, because redemption had not been accomplished then. The author says after that, concerning the body, that is the Church:

> He officially consecrated it [i.e. His body] to the Church on the cross, when He anointed it with the anointing of redemption, with the blood of God which was poured on it, so the Church was sanctified forever to the account of God, considering that she is His body which He took from us, sanctified it, redeemed it, and granted it to us with all His Divine attributes as the body of the Son of God.

8. Was the Church sanctified when she was consecrated by the blood on the cross?

---

506 See Luke 1:45.
507 See Acts 2.

Or was she sanctified on the day she was born in Baptism by regeneration[508]? Or was she sanctified by Holy Myron in the Mystery of the Holy Anointing? Or was she holy from the womb through her uniting with the Divinity, according to the author's opinion? And was the Church, which was born united with the Divinity, according to his opinion, in need of consecration and sanctification?

As for his saying, "The Church was sanctified forever for God's account, considering that she is His body which He took from us, sanctified it, redeemed it, and granted it to us with all His Divine attributes as the body of the Son of God," so, is she His body which He took from us, or He took from Virgin Mary, if it were the body of the whole redeemed humanity?

And what does the following mean, "[He] granted it to us with all His Divine attributes, as the body of the Son of God, bestowing it to her after He completed in it His lifting up to the highest heavens, to join His eternal attributes to her account"? What are all these Divine attributes and eternal attributes which Christ bestowed upon the Church? Does this mean the deification of the Church? And how does He grant His body to her, here, and she is His body?

9. What is the meaning of "We became of His flesh and His bones"?

The author says, "In this manner, Christ fed us His body and blood which came out of His side, so we became of His flesh and His bones." The term "of His flesh and His bones" he repeats in two of his books. At this the reader is perplexed, did we become of His flesh and His bones when we became a Church which Christ loved as Adam loved his wife because she was his flesh and his bones? Or did we become of His flesh and His bones when He redeemed us? Or did we become of His flesh and His bones when we were born in Bethlehem, as he says? Or did we become of His flesh and His bones

---

508 See Titus 3:5.

when He shared with us in human nature in His Incarnation?[509] This is confusion, which complicates the theological though!

10. What is the meaning of "uniting the Divine nature with the human nature"?

The Divine nature was united with the human nature in the womb of the Virgin. That is, it was united with the humanity of Christ, and not with the Church, which is the bride. But the author says, "The image of the bridegroom and the bride and the one flesh, all these go back to their first source, which is mystical to the uttermost, when the Word became flesh. For the Divine nature was united with the human in an eternal, inseparable matrimony."

Was this eternal matrimony with the Church or with His humanity? Or does the author see that Christ's humanity and the Church are one being? The day the Word became flesh, there was no Church. What is then the meaning of matrimony here? And what does the image of the Bridegroom and the Church as the bride have to do with the Divine Incarnation? It is neither possible nor logical that we say that the bride of Christ is His humanity which was born of the Virgin Mary; nor that the Divinity of Christ was united with His humanity in an eternal matrimony. And this is not the intention of the author in speaking of the Church as a bride.

11. Confusing between two meanings of the body of Christ

The author continues to confuse the Church with the body of Christ, which was born of the Virgin, saying "Christ, the Baby of the manger, was Himself the Church of the cradle, and on the cross, He became the Church of the redemption stained with blood, and on the third day, He is the Church of the resurrection." He is as though saying that it is not Christ who was born, was crucified and rose, but it is the Church that was born in the cradle, and it is [the

---

509 See Hebrews 2:14.

Church] on the cross stained with blood, and it is [the Church] in the resurrection!

Notes against this confusion

✢ The body of Christ that was born of the Virgin is a true body, with the literal meaning of the word, but the Church is considered the body of Christ with a spiritual meaning, not literally. There are many differences between these two uses of the term "the body of Christ," which we will mention. Therefore, we should not confuse between them.

✢ The body of Christ was born of the Virgin St. Mary, while the body of Christ meaning the Church means the congregation of the believers. So, is it plausible to say concerning millions of believers who lived in many successive generations that they were too born of the Virgin Mary?

✢ The body of Christ that was of the Virgin is that which we partake of in Communion from the altar, according to the word of the Lord who said, "This is My body."[510] This does not apply to the body of Christ meaning the Church, because we do not partake of the Church in Communion.

✢ The body of Christ that was born of the Virgin we worship in the Mystery of the Eucharist, saying, "We worship Your holy Body, Lord." But we do not worship the Church; for we are the Church.

✢ The body of Christ on the cross is that which redeemed us. So if the Church were the body of Christ with the same meaning too, would we attribute to her the redemption of humankind?

✢ The body of Christ is united with His Divinity permanently, and has not parted from it for a single moment, nor a twinkling of an eye. So, is the Church united likewise with the Divinity, without mingling, without confusion, and without alteration, and is not separated from [the Divinity] for a single moment?

---

510 Matthew 26:26.

✤ The body of Christ that is born of the Virgin is a perfect body, while the body meaning the Church has not reached perfection yet, but new members who are not born yet will join it, and others of the unbelievers will join the faith, and consequently [join] the body of the Church.

✤ The body of Christ meaning the Church means the believers who are of [various] levels and kinds. Some of them are living the life of righteousness; some others are striving to reach [perfection], who fall and stand up again, but have not been crowned yet. But the body of Christ that is born of the Virgin is a holy and glorified body, and it helps us in our striving.

✤ Had the Church been the body of Christ which is on the altar and at the right hand of the Father in heaven, this thought would have led us to the heresy of Pantheism into which many of the heretical philosophers fell.

✤ None of the [Church] Fathers said that Christ is the Church. But the Scripture said that He is the head of the Church.[511] As for the Church, she is the body, which includes many members who are the congregation of the believers.

✤ Confusing between the body of Christ that is born of the Virgin and the body of Christ that is the Church leads to the consideration that the Church is an extension of the Divine Incarnation, as it came in the author's book. Therefore, confusing between these two uses of the term "the body of Christ" is not permitted, to avoid the aforementioned issues.

12. What is the meaning of the mystical body of Christ which fills heaven and earth?

It is known that God alone is He who fills heaven and earth. Because God is infinite, He is present in every place. And there is none other who is infinite, for we are all finite. If the Church is meant by the mystical body of Christ, according to the opinion of the writer in all his publications, she cannot fill heaven and earth.

---

511 See Ephesians 5:23.

She is truly present on earth but cannot fill all the earth. And some of her children are in heaven, but they do not fill heaven. And if the body of Christ that is born of the Virgin is meant by the mystical body of Christ, how is it said that it is a mystical body?

13. Are we in Baptism made from the mystical body of Christ?

What is the meaning of the author's saying in one of his books under the heading, "The Holy Spirit the Maker of our new temples and the One who brings them into existence"?

> In Baptism, of whom are we born, and according to what form is our new man? The Holy Spirit is He who makes the temple of our new man. He makes it from the mystical body of Christ which fills heaven and earth.

Then he speaks about the body of Christ with which He entered the upper room, and the doors were shut. And he says, "We are born of this flesh and these same bones," and, "We are of His flesh and His bones." Is it plausible that in Baptism we are born of the flesh of Christ and His bones, with which He entered the upper room, and the doors were shut? That is, of His body which is born of Virgin Mary? Or, as it came in his book, that we are born with Christ of the womb of Virgin Mary.

Then he says, "The Holy Spirit creates this new temple from the invisible body. And after He creates it, He fills it: 'You are the temple of God and that the Spirit of God dwells in you.'" So, is Baptism an act of new birth or an act of creation? What is the meaning of "The Holy Spirit creates this new temple from the invisible body"? Is this invisible body, the body of Christ? How is it invisible? Or, is this invisible body, the body of the Church? And if it is so, how is the phrase "of this flesh and these same bones" applied to it?

He also says in one of his books, "Christ, of His flesh and bones, everyday creates the new, spiritual man, whom He supports with the blessing of the New Testament." All that we have learned from the Church is that in Baptism we are born of water and the Spirit, without mentioning flesh or bones, and without mentioning a mystical body or an invisible body we are born of. And so long as we are born in Baptism, this means that we were not born in Bethlehem, as the author says in his book. And consequently, we were not born of the womb of the Virgin, being of the members of the Church or the redeemed humanity.

14. Is the mystical body of Christ the one in the [Mystery of the] Eucharist?

The author, however, gives another meaning for "the mystical body of Christ," saying in his book concerning what happened on the day of Pentecost:

> The descent of the Holy Spirit, then, on the day of Pentecost does not point to the bestowal of a mere spiritual power, nor the bestowal of gifts and talents, randomly. Rather, the matter is very serious, for here there is a mystical sign that an invisible union took place between a Divine nature and a human nature. And what would that Divine nature be except the mystical body of Christ itself, which Christ had before pointed to taking it, eating it, uniting with it, and abiding in it.

If the Divine nature is the body of Christ, where then is the Divinity and where is the humanity? It is as though he is saying that the Divinity is Itself the humanity! And is the mystical body of Christ that which we partake of in the Mystery of the Eucharist? This is another meaning for "the mystical body of Christ" which the author presents. By bringing together this idea and the previous one, how are we born of this body in Baptism, according to his saying, "The Holy Spirit is He who makes the temple of our new man. He makes it from the mystical body of Christ which fills heaven and earth"?

It is a confounding matter, undoubtedly. This mystical body of Christ, according to the author's explanation, is it the body of

Christ that was born of the Virgin, in His flesh and bones? Or is it the Church, the body of Christ? Or is it His body in the Mystery of the Eucharist?

In one of his books he asks this question and answers it, saying, "But what is the connection between mystical body of Christ in the Church and His body in heaven sitting at the right hand of God? It is a single body, without separation in heaven and on earth."

The definitions of the mystical body of Christ remain discrepant with each other, for the body sitting at the right hand of God is the body that was born of the Virgin, which is united with the Divinity; and this is *not* the Church in any way whatsoever. For the Church is the body of Christ, not in the literal meaning, and is not the body that was born of the Virgin.

15. On Pentecost, was a Divine nature united with a human nature?

As for his saying that on Pentecost "union took place between a Divine nature and a human nature," in which the disciples represent the whole Church, this matter cannot be theologically accepted at all. The only One, in whom the Divine nature was united with human nature, is the Lord Christ, the incarnate God, and not the Apostles. Impossible.

Here I would like to say that there are two ways to attack the Divinity of Christ: First, the Arian teaching, in which Christ is lowered to the human level; second, the deification of man, in which men are lifted up to the level of Christ. The aforementioned is an example of the latter case, in which it is said that on Pentecost a union took place in the disciples between a Divine nature and a human nature. What is the difference then between them and the Lord Christ? No difference, and this is what the author says in his book.

16. Was that which began in Bethlehem completed in the upper room?

He says concerning the descent of the Holy Spirit on Pentecost:

> The Holy Spirit did not descend in the form of a dove amidst the water of the Jordan to give the power of Baptism through water and Spirit, but descended as tongues as though of fire, and sat upon each of them. Then we are [standing] before a "bush burning with fire," according to the symbol; or a Divine nature united with a human nature, according to the explanation of the symbol; or the image of the prophecy of the Nativity of Christ, as we have received [it] from Holy Tradition!

He sees that what happened to the Apostles represents the whole Church, saying, "The purpose of the Divine Incarnation reached its pinnacle on the day of Pentecost." The Divine Incarnation is a Divine nature united with a human nature. So, did this reach its pinnacle on the day of Pentecost, when the same thing happened with respect to the Apostles, according to his saying? Or, to the whole Church?

Yes, he says, "What was started in Bethlehem happened and was completed in the upper room." What was started in Bethlehem is the Divine Incarnation, in which the Divine nature was united with human nature in the Person of Christ. So, did this happen and was it completed in the upper room on the day of Pentecost, with the Apostles representing the Church, all becoming perfectly like Christ?

17. Did the Church acquire all that belongs to Christ?

He says immediately before this under the heading "The form in which the Holy Spirit descended on the day of Pentecost," "Christ united with the Church, so the Church acquired all that belongs to Christ." After this he says under the heading, "The Holy Spirit is the Maker of our new temples," "The fundamental work of the Holy Spirit in our new man is giving us all that belongs to Christ, that we may become fitting for the permanent union with Him."

How dangerous is the word "all" in theological expressions!

The Church did not acquire all that belongs to Christ, for Christ has Divinity which the Church did not acquire. To Christ belong divine attributes like eternity[512], infinity, the power to create, and absolute authority—and the Church has acquired none of these. And Christ has a relationship with the Father, of which He said, "I and My Father are one,"[513] and, "He who has seen Me has seen the Father"[514]—and this also the Church has not acquired. And so is the case with all the glory of the Divinity which belongs to Christ.

We can say that Christ gave us of what is His, of His human attributes which we can attain. As for the term "all that belongs to Christ," it is absolutely impossible for us to reach; it is a term that is not acceptable theologically. Likewise in Baptism, the Holy Spirit did not give us all that belongs to Christ.

Sadly, the author repeats the same phrase, which he said in one of his books, in another of his books, saying, "What happened on Pentecost is the union of a Divine nature with human nature," and he says, "And what would that Divine nature be except the mystical body of Christ itself, which Christ had before pointed to taking it, eating it, uniting with it." He also spoke about receiving the Holy Spirit as a hypostasis. He also said, "The purpose of the Divine Incarnation reached its pinnacle on the day of Pentecost," and said, "Christ united with the Church, so the Church acquired all that belongs to Christ… That which began in Bethlehem happened and was completed in the upper room," and said also, "The Divine body which is expressed as the fullness of the Godhead bodily."

Indeed, that which he wrote in 1960 he literally repeated in 1988. It is an insistence on an understanding[515] which must be faced.

18. Does the Holy Spirit fashion us in the nature of the Son of God?

---

512 Arabic: *al-azalia*, i.e. without beginning, existing from everlasting.
513 John 10:30.
514 John 14:9.
515 Or: thought.

The author continues his understanding with another similar statement: "Therefore, after the Holy Spirit begets us in Baptism and fashions us in the nature of the Son of God, He cannot but bear witness to our spirits that we are sons of God." And here we stand before the statement "fashions us in the nature of the Son of God." The nature of the Son of God is perfect Divinity united with perfect humanity. This is the nature of the incarnate Word. So, how does the Holy Spirit fashion us in this nature? All that could be said is that He brings us close to the image of His humanity, making us conformed to the perfection of humanity, to that which our human nature is able to reach through the help of grace. He makes us "conformed to the image of His Son."[516]

As for fashioning us in the nature of the Son of God, this is impossible theologically. Our human nature will remain the same, but with purity and renewing. And the nature of the Son of God will remain the same: perfect Divinity united with holy, perfect humanity.

19. Our sonship to God and the sonship of the Lord Christ to God.

We truly become sons of God, but not in the nature of the Son of God. For He is the Son of God in a manner[517], and we are sons of God in another manner. Therefore, it was written of Him that He is "the only begotten Son of God."[518] As for our sonship, it is a sort[519] of adoption.[520] John the Apostle said concerning the Lord Christ, "But as many as received Him, to them He gave the right to become children of God, to those who believe in His name."[521] And he said, "Behold what manner of love the Father has bestowed on us, that we should be called children of God!"[522]

---

516 Romans 8:29.
517 Literally: meaning.
518 John 3:16, 18; 1 John 4:9; John 1:18.
519 Literally: tinge.
520 See Galatians 4:5; Romans 8:23.
521 John 1:12.
522 1 John 3:1.

Then our sonship to God is a kind of love or adoption or faith, and absolutely not because we were fashioned in the nature of the Son of God.

20. What is the meaning of "We have become a Christ"?

The author uses a quote, out of context, by St. Augustine, saying, "We have not only become Christians, but have become a Christ."[523] St. Augustine was saying that the Lord Christ considered us as Himself. For He said to Saul of Tarsus, "Why are you persecuting Me?"[524] and not, "Why are you persecuting the members of the Church?" For as though we are Him. And likewise in caring for the poor, He said, "For I was hungry and you gave Me food; I was thirsty and you gave Me drink…"[525] and He said after this, "Assuredly, I say to you, inasmuch as you did it to one of the least of these My brethren, you did it to Me."[526] This is what St. Augustine meant, but he was not speaking of the theological meaning, nor that we have come to have the nature of Christ—God forbid!

On this occasion, we reiterate that using the sayings of the Fathers with an understanding, and on an occasion, not their own, is a matter that causes offence and has its dangers. We must not then use the sayings of the Fathers to mean what they did not intend, altering them to mean something else.

21. Is the Divine body all the fullness of the Godhead bodily?

The author pursues his intended understanding concerning Pentecost, saying, "The Divine body which is expressed as 'the fullness of the Godhead bodily,'[527] we have become fully filled in Him since Pentecost."

---

523 See Augustine *Homilies on the Gospel of John* XXI.V(20–23).8 (NPNF[1] 7:140).
524 Acts 9:4.
525 Matthew 25:35.
526 Matthew 25:40.
527 Colossians 2:9.

It is impossible that the Divine body is expressed as the fullness of the Godhead! For if the body is the fullness of the Godhead, where then is the humanity? Where is the Divinity? The verse says, "And not according to Christ. For in Him dwells all the fullness of the Godhead bodily."[528] There is a an extremely vast difference between the expression "For in Him dwells all the fullness of the Godhead bodily" and "The Divine body is all the fullness of the Godhead bodily."

This confusion between the Divinity and humanity—as though the nature of each of them is lost or is dissolved in the other nature—reminds us also of his saying on the same subject, "And what would that Divine nature be except the mystical body of Christ itself." He says that the Divine nature is the mystical body of Christ, and he says that the Divine body is the fullness of the Godhead bodily! So, is the Divine nature the human nature, according to his saying?

We see astonishing things in all these explanations, which are against the theological teaching of the Church.

---

528 Colossians 2:8–9.

CHAPTER ELEVEN

The War Against the Law and Works

Introduction

The author has violently attacked the Law and works in his book on Paul the Apostle and in his explanation of the epistle to the Romans. But I have not found in any other book of his such an attack on the Law as in his explanation of the epistle to the Galatians, in which he mentioned that the Law was abolished, sin was abolished, punishments were abolished, death was abolished, the commandments were abolished, the curse was abolished. He also spoke of the free-of-charge salvation, free-of-charge righteousness, free-of-charge remission, free-of-charge holiness, free-of-charge new creation, free-of-charge eternal life, and so on. And he spoke against works and attacked them, and said that we stand before the Law sinless, for it has no case against us; and that God has forgiven us all the previous and the coming sins which we will commit in the future. He said also that God asks nothing of man except faith only, and even this faith is a gift from God, and grace abolishes works.

We will explain and discuss this thought [or understanding] in detail in the following sections.

1. What does the Holy Scriptures mean by "the Law"?

The word *nomos* (νόμος) means law, and it includes all the decrees and commandments of God, including those found in the Five Books of Moses, which are called the Law. Also included are the divine commandments that came in the books of the prophets and in the New Testament as well. Some of these commandments were a symbol that was replaced by that which they symbolized. Of such symbols are the animal sacrifices which were replaced by the sacrifice of Christ; and of such is the Passover, about which it is said, "For indeed Christ, our Passover, was sacrificed for us."[529]

There are also the works of the Law, like the old feasts[530] and the matters that concern uncleanness and purification. All these were symbols, about which St. Paul said, "So let no one judge you in food or in drink, or regarding a festival or a new moon or sabbaths, which are a shadow of things to come, but the substance is of Christ."[531]

As for the rest of the Law, it consists of divine commandments, of which David the prophet sang, saying, "The law of the LORD is perfect, converting the soul; the testimony of the LORD is sure, making wise the simple; the statutes of the LORD are right, rejoicing the heart; … the judgments of the LORD are true and righteous altogether. More to be desired are they than gold, yea, than much fine gold; sweeter also than honey and the honeycomb."[532] David the prophet also said, "His delight is in the law of the LORD, and in His law, he meditates day and night."[533] We sing these every day in the First Hour [of Agpeya]. We also sing in the Midnight Prayer that which David the prophet mentioned in the Great Psalm (Psalm 119) concerning the Lord's testimonies, judgments, and His Law, saying, "Your word is a lamp to my feet and a light to my path;"[534] "For Your law is my delight;"[535] "I will keep Your precepts with my whole heart;"[536] "Seven times a day I praise You, because of Your righteous judgments."[537]

---

[529] 1 Corinthians 5:7.
[530] See Leviticus 23.
[531] Colossians 2:16–17.
[532] Psalms 19:7–10.
[533] Psalms 1:2.
[534] Psalms 119:105.
[535] Psalms 119:77.
[536] Psalms 119:69.
[537] Psalms 119:164.

After examining these points, we now address the following critical question.

2. Did God abolish the commandments and all the judgments of the Law?

The Lord says to us in the Sermon on the Mount, "Do not think that I came to destroy the Law or the Prophets. I did not come to destroy but to fulfill. For assuredly, I say to you, till heaven and earth pass away, one jot or one tittle will by no means pass from the law till all is fulfilled."[538]

The author, however, of the explanation of the epistle to the Galatians says, "So, by the coming of faith, Christ opened the prison of sins, annulled sin by the sacrifice of Himself, stopped the Law from its authority which gave orders [to put man] to death, abolished the law of punishments, and cancelled death." And he also says, "It is known that whoever commits sin dies. For the power of sin, which made it dreadful and gave it significance and presence, is the punishment of death, being the inevitable punishment of sin. For if God abolished the punishment of death, sin was unquestionably abolished. And consequently, all the judgments of the Law were abolished, and the Law lost its necessity, and lost its presence, without touching the reverence for the word of God."

So how does the Law lose its necessity, presence, and judgments, without touching the reverence for the word of God, while the Law is the word of God? Is there not contradiction in this?

The author also says in his interpretation of Romans, "From now on there is no Law at all, but a release and cutting the bonds asunder." After all this, we can ask the following.

3. Was sin abolished? And was the punishment of death abolished?

Sin was not abolished. For Paul the Apostle himself says, "I agree

---

538 Matthew 5:17–18.

with the law that it is good. But now, it is no longer I who do it, but sin that dwells in me.... Now if I do what I will not to do, it is no longer I who do it, but sin that dwells in me."[539] "For we know that the law is spiritual, but I am carnal, sold under sin."[540] So how is it said that "sin was abolished"?

St. John says in his first epistle, "If we say that we have no sin, we deceive ourselves, and the truth is not in us."[541] St. Paul the Apostle says also, "Christ Jesus came into the world to save sinners, of whom I am chief."[542] Then, there is sin, and there is death too. So how does the author say that God has abolished sin fully and has abolished the punishment of death?

The punishment of death is present, as it came in the book of Ezekiel the prophet, "The soul who sins shall die."[543] For God has not abolished the punishment of death, but He bore it instead of us on the cross. And the everlasting death is still present as a punishment for sinners. This is not the teaching of the Old Testament only, but is mentioned in the New Testament also: "For the wages of sin is death."[544]

Nevertheless, the author, in his explanation of the epistle to the Galatians, says, "The banner of the New Testament has become the remission of sins and the bestowal of eternal life, through the blood of Christ freely[545], in place of the old banner through the fulfillment of all the commandments, and everyone who sins dies." So, has this old banner ended then, and we are no longer required to fulfill all the commandments? And is death no longer the punishment of sin?[546]

Was the law of punishments abolished as he says? We have before us a long list in Corinthians (6:9–10) concerning

---

539 Romans 7:16–17, 20.
540 Romans 7:14.
541 1 John 1:8.
542 1 Timothy 1:15.
543 Ezekiel 18:4, 20.
544 Romans 6:23.
545 Or: free of charge.
546 See Romans 6:23.

punishment which forbids entrance into the Kingdom of God, and another indication in Romans (2:3–6) concerning punishment: "Treasuring up for yourself wrath in the day of wrath and revelation of the righteous judgment of God, who 'will render to each one according to his deeds.'"[547]

So, is it, after all these, said with all boldness that God has abolished the law of punishments, canceled death, abolished death, and stopped the Law?

And does the giving of eternal life free of charge mean exemption from repentance and good works? In all the author's words concerning free-of-charge salvation and free-of-charge righteousness, he has said nothing about the necessity of repentance. And look, the Lord Christ says, "Unless you repent you will all likewise perish."[548] And does giving us redemption freely by the blood of Christ, according to the statement "being justified freely by His grace," mean the omission of repentance, the commandments and the Law, and good works?

The author says in the explanation of the epistle to the Galatians, "In order for God to end the Law and the commandments utterly, He abolished all sins, but even abolished the nature of sin and its power, which is the power of the Law. So, the Law lost, and the commandments lost their power, that is their work utterly, consequently their existence." Do Christians currently live without commandments, in that God has ended the commandments, as the author says, and that the commandments lost their power and existence? Consequently, were the Sermon on the Mount and all the teachings of Christ abolished? And were all the commandments abolished in Romans 12, 1 Corinthians 13, and in all the teaching of the holy Apostles? Look, the Lord Christ says, "He who has My commandments and keeps them, it is he who loves Me."[549] He also says, "But everyone who hears these sayings of Mine, and does not do them, will be like a foolish man who built his house on the

---

547   Romans 2:5–6.
548   Luke 13:3, 5.
549   John 14:21; see also John 14:15.

sand.... and it fell. And great was its fall."[550] So, how is it said then that God has ended the commandments and abolished them?

4. Did the Law push St. Paul to madly commit crimes?

The author says in his book about St. Paul, "The Law pushed him to commit the most heinous crimes," and he also says, "It pushed him to kill the believers and torture them, and persecute the Church madly." The use of the terms "the most heinous crimes" and "madly" are not fitting at all when speaking of a great saint like Paul the Apostle. It is true that he persecuted the Church, and on this he says, "But I obtained mercy because I did it ignorantly in unbelief."[551] It is not the Law then that pushed Saul of Tarsus to persecute the Church, that he [i.e. the author] may attack the Law, but ignorance and unbelief pushed him; that is, ignorance of the matter of redemption and salvation, and unbelief, *at that time*, that Jesus of Nazareth is the Messiah who carries the sins of the world and saves it.

5. Does God seek nothing of man except faith alone?

In his explanation of the epistle to the Galatians, the author spoke at length about grace and faith, with belittlement of works, as though he says, "all through grace; all through faith," according to what he says, "Christ seeks nothing of man except his faith... and then he is in the sphere of the power of Christ who fulfills everything for him. And he no longer has any work except understanding the work of Christ and rejoicing in it."

For our understanding of the teaching of the Scripture to be holistic, we must put next to faith the sayings St. James the Apostle: "For as the body without the spirit is dead, so faith without works is dead also;"[552] "Thus also faith by itself, if it does not have works, is dead;"[553] "What does it profit, my brethren, if someone says he

---

550 Matthew 7:26–27.
551 1 Timothy 1:13.
552 James 2:26.
553 James 2:17.

has faith but does not have works? Can faith save him?"[554] But the author abolishes works in his speaking about grace.

6. Does grace abolish works, and works abolish grace?

In his explanation of the epistle to the Galatians, the author says:

> St. Paul, in his epistle to the Galatians, places the firm foundation for the work of grace and for works, and the separation between them, for each one of them abolishes the other. For grace abolishes works, and vice versa, works abolish grace. And this is the great danger not only to the faith of the Galatians, but to our faith in the grace of Christ which does not accept the addition of any work whatever, not even the chopping of the body. St. Paul distilled it in his epistle to the Romans in this manner: "Being justified freely by His grace through the redemption that is in Christ Jesus."[555] Also, "For by grace you have been saved through faith, and that not of yourselves; it is the gift of God."[556] Therefore, the saying of St. Paul in his epistle to the Galatians—"You have become estranged from Christ, you who attempt to be justified by law; you have fallen from grace"[557]—is considered the foundation of the gospel of St. Paul, which he preached to Jews and Gentiles alike, and consequently, the foundation of all the epistles.

7. What is the sound explanation of the teaching of St. Paul?

In his sayings "Being justified freely by His grace" and "By grace you have been saved," St. Paul means the redemption which cannot be replaced with human work. Therefore, he said, "Being justified freely by His grace through the redemption that is in Christ

---

554 James 2:14.
555 Romans 3:24.
556 Ephesians 2:8.
557 Galatians 5:4.

Jesus."[558] And his saying "For by grace you have been saved through faith,"[559] means through faith in the redemption, in the work of Christ on the cross. And this redemption is "not of yourselves; it is the gift of God."[560]

But the mere faith in the redemption must be followed by other works, such as repentance, Baptism, good works, and walking in the Spirit. For the Jews, in whom grace worked on Pentecost, who were cut to the heart and believed, were not satisfied with faith and grace, but said to the Apostles, "'Men and brethren, what shall we do?' Then Peter said to them, 'Repent, and let every one of you be baptized in the name of Jesus Christ for the remission of sins; and you shall receive the gift of the Holy Spirit.'"[561] He did not say to them, "Christ seeks nothing of man except his faith," as the author says.

Yet [even] the Lord Christ Himself says at the end of the Gospel according to St. Mark, "He who believes and is baptized will be saved."[562] He also says about repentance, "Unless you repent you will all likewise perish."[563] Faith is a first step which must be followed by other steps. The author, however, speaks about the salvation of ungodly and profane men.

8. Can the ungodly be justified before God?

In the explanation of the same epistle, the author says:

> But God's calling through the grace of Christ means directly and with power to a salvific work, which is accomplished and was accomplished by the redemptive death of Christ, that this redemptive work may course through the ungodly, the unworthy, and the profane—through faith to justify him by the righteousness of God. So, the ungodly is

---

558   Romans 3:24.
559   Ephesians 2:8.
560   Ephesians 2:8.
561   Acts 2:37–38.
562   Mark 16:16.
563   Luke 13:3.

justified in the eyes of God, is reconciled, and receives the adoption! For if God has called them through the grace of Christ, they have entered into the perfect righteousness of God, where the righteousness of God cannot be increased by works; otherwise, the relying on works abolishes the righteousness of God.

It is clear that God does not justify the ungodly unless he repents. And as our teacher St. Peter the Apostle said, "If the righteous one is scarcely saved, where will the ungodly and the sinner appear?"[564] St. Paul the Apostle himself says in his epistle to the Romans, "For the wrath of God is revealed from heaven against all ungodliness and unrighteousness of men,"[565] and says in his first epistle to the Corinthians that such as these will not inherit the kingdom of God.[566]

Very sadly however, the author, throughout this subject, did not make any mention that repentance is a condition for the acceptance of the ungodly, but goes further by justifying the profane and the unworthy. And the term "unworthy" is dangerous, because without repentance every sinner is unworthy of justification, so how much more the one who is profane.

9. What are the limits of the word "freely" in the author's writings?

He focuses on the word "freely" in the expression "Being justified freely"[567] and adds to it, "For by grace you have been saved through faith ...not of works, lest anyone should boast,"[568] even though the following comes after, "For we are His workmanship, created in Christ Jesus for good works, which God prepared beforehand that we should walk in them."[569] Nevertheless, the author focuses on the

---

564 1 Peter 4:18.
565 Romans 1:18.
566 See 1 Corinthians 6:9–10.
567 Romans 3:24.
568 Ephesians 2:8–9.
569 Ephesians 2:10.

word "freely" and says, "The word 'freely' is capable per se to bring back the one who is in despair, that he may rise and preach the free salvation."

He says also, "The grace of Christ has granted you eternal life freely, so seize grace, hold onto it and wager on it. It is able by itself to make you inherit eternal life. Grace was registered in heaven to your account the day you believed in Christ, so do not think that you need anything or anyone to bring it down from heaven to you… thus does the epistle to the Galatians declare concerning the outcry of grace in the face of the Christian man: Receive the freedom with which Christ freed you, to live for God."

Researching what is meant by "freely."

Christ offered us redemption through His blood "freely," yet with conditions. The first condition is faith. As the Scripture says, "that whoever believes in Him should not perish but have everlasting life,"[570] and it says also, "He who believes in the Son has everlasting life; and he who does not believe the Son shall not see life, but the wrath of God abides on him."[571] So what is the meaning of the author's saying, "The grace of Christ has granted you eternal life freely," and concerning faith he says, "Thus there is no work in existence that may qualify us for the gift of faith, or make us worthy of the grace of Christ. For faith is a gift, and grace is a right for everyone who believes." So, if faith were a gift, what would be the distinction between the believer and unbeliever, if there were no work in existence that may qualify us for the gift of faith?

The second and third conditions are repentance and Baptism, as St. Peter the Apostle said on Pentecost, "Repent, and let every one of you be baptized in the name of Jesus Christ for the remission of sins."[572]

The fourth condition is good works and walking in the Spirit, according to St. Paul the Apostle's saying, "There is therefore now

---

570 John 3:16.
571 John 3:36.
572 Acts 2:38.

no condemnation to those who are in Christ Jesus, who do not walk according to the flesh, but according to the Spirit,"[573] and according the saying of James the Apostle, "That faith without works is dead."[574]

Undoubtedly, these four conditions are all works.

The author, however, says in his explanation of the epistle to the Galatians:

> So, does the gospel of Christ need complementation of any sort, **whether by the works of the Law and others**? With all truth and certainty, the work of Christ is divine, transcendent, and nothing can be added to it, and it does not need human complementation **of any sort**. Otherwise, the work of the Son of God would be considered incomplete, requiring complementation through the works of man, whether through the decree of the Old Law or through the rebuke of the deficient, skeptical conscience. This is considered straying from the true Gospel or the truth of the Gospel, or is considered as though it is another Gospel!
>
> For if the redeemed man, who has received salvation, turned away from the gospel of his salvation toward the works of the Law or the works of the thought, the conscience, or the body, as though they were necessary to complete his salvation, he would have gone out of the limits of the truth of the gospel; and consequently, he would have fallen from the grace of the faith in Christ, as St. Paul says in the same epistle.... For any turning towards **the works of the Law or any other works**, as though they are necessary for salvation, Paul the Apostle considers that falling from grace, and consequently from the faith in Christ and the redemptive works of Christ. [See Galatians 5:4].... There is no necessity for those who have believed in Christ and His redemptive works of suffering and death, that they do any work, whether great

---

573 Romans 8:1.
574 James 2:20. Also see James 2:17.

or small, to add to their faith in Christ and His works, to be worthy of remission of sins or salvation.

10. There is a difference between the work of redemption and being worthy of redemption.

The work of redemption the Lord Christ accomplished alone; this is a matter in which there is no addition. Did all people, however, benefit from this great redemption? Look, St. Paul the Apostle says, "How shall we escape if we neglect so great a salvation?"[575] What about those who believed yet walked in sin, and did not repent? What about those who believed in the redemption yet partook of the body and blood of the Lord unworthily, so, by that, they partook judgment to themselves?[576] What about those who believed, whom St. Paul mentioned in his epistles, and then he said, "For many walk, of whom I have told you often, and now tell you even weeping, that they are the enemies of the cross of Christ: whose end is destruction, whose god is their belly, and whose glory is in their shame—who set their mind on earthly things."[577] And what about those who believed and became shepherds and leaders of the Church, but they erred in the doctrine and were excommunicated by the holy Councils? Were these worthy of the blood of the Redeemer?

How is it that after all this we do not talk about the importance of works, while God will come in His glory, "to reward each according to his works,"[578] "whether good or bad"[579]? We note that the author did not attack the works of the Law only, like circumcision, the Sabbath, and Jewish ordinances,[580] but every work whether great or small, whether of the works of the thought, conscience, or body! And he said that this is another gospel or a straying from the truth

---

575 Hebrews 2:3.
576 See 1 Corinthians 11:29.
577 Philippians 3:18–19.
578 Matthew 16:27.
579 2 Corinthians 5:10.
580 See Colossians 2:16–17.

of the gospel, as though they were complementing the redemptive work of Christ, and not out of worthiness.

I wish that we remember, besides faith, that which was said concerning the awesome Judgment Day, that the Lord will cast out those who did not feed the hungry, did not give water to the thirsty, did not visit the sick, although they said to Him, "Lord."[581] These, however, went away into everlasting punishment.[582]

I wish that we remember the foolish virgins, against whom the Lord's door was shut, so they did not enter, although they were believers, waited for the bridegroom, and said to Him, "Lord, Lord, open to us!"[583] Their problem was that they did not take oil [with their lamps].

As for the accusation that works are a complementation of Christ's work of salvation, for although works are for the mere worthiness, we place beside them the saying of Paul the Apostle himself: "Work out your own salvation with fear and trembling."[584] The salvation, which the Lord offered on the cross, we need to fulfill in our practical life, according to the teaching this [same] Apostle who called for the free salvation. This is not by partaking in the redemptive suffering of Christ, as the author said in some of his writings, but it is by persistence in repentance, assiduousness, diligence, resisting sin and the enemy of good, continuance in spiritual vigilance, and so on. And all these are works.

11. How do we fulfill our salvation, according to the teaching of the Scriptures?

We fulfill it by the works of repentance, according to the warning of the Lord, which He said, twice, "Unless you repent you will all likewise perish,"[585] and according to the saying in the book of Acts,

---

581 Matthew 25:41.
582 Matthew 25:46.
583 Matthew 25:11.
584 Philippians 2:12.
585 Luke 13:3 and 13:5.

"God has also granted to the Gentiles repentance to life."[586]

Repentance requires struggle, spiritual vigilance, and resisting the devil. As St. Peter the Apostle said, "Be sober, be vigilant; because your adversary the devil walks about like a roaring lion, seeking whom he may devour. Resist him, steadfast in the faith, knowing that the same sufferings are experienced by your brotherhood in the world."[587] And as St. Paul the Apostle rebuked the Hebrews, saying, "You have not yet resisted to bloodshed, striving against sin."[588] And concerning vigilance, the Lord said, "Blessed are those servants whom the master, when he comes, will find watching."[589] "Let your waist be girded and your lamps burning."[590] "Therefore you also be ready, for the Son of Man is coming at an hour you do not expect."[591]

Nevertheless, the author says in his explanation of the epistle to the Galatians:

> It is necessary for man to eliminate[592] that which has precipitated in his mind, over these years, but over these generations, of his pressing need to satisfy God with works.... Is the Christian man, who has believed in Christ, has received the righteousness and free remission, and has entered with God into reconciliation and fellowship of eternal life—is he not considered blaspheming against the cross and the free Christian remission, but even [is considered] ridiculing the Christian faith, if he thinks that by the works he does—such as fasting and almsgiving, keeping vigil and beating the chest, worshipping and humility, lowering oneself even to the dust—he is justified before God, or is approved of God and approaches [Him] by them? For man is not justified by works at all, but is

---

586 Acts 11:18.
587 1 Peter 5:8–9.
588 Hebrews 12:4.
589 Luke 12:37.
590 Luke 12:35.
591 Luke 12:40.
592 Literally: take off.

justified by faith in Christ. And faith in Christ is only approved before God: "For the Father Himself loves you, because you have loved Me, and have believed that I came forth from God" (John 16:27).

It makes one marvel at how worthless this spiritual struggle[593] is before the author. What about then the monastic spiritual struggle, prostrations, keeping vigil at night, and what we read in the accounts of the desert fathers and their struggles? What about our fasting and prostrations in this Holy Great Fast? What about the asceticism and struggle of the people of Nineveh, with which they pleased God, so He lifted His wrath away from them?

It is worthy to note that in the previous quote he was not speaking of the works of the Law and Jewish ordinances [only], but even of our current form of worship.

12. Do these words apply to the teaching of Paul the Apostle and his life?

It makes one marvel that the author says such a statement in his explanation of an epistle of St. Paul the Apostle who [himself] said, "I discipline my body and bring it into subjection, lest, when I have preached to others, I myself should become disqualified."[594] Why do you, O great and humble saint, discipline your body and bring it into subjection? Have you not received free salvation and free righteousness, by your believing in Christ? What is the meaning of the phrase that I myself should become disqualified?

And concerning the striving, St. Paul the Apostle in his last days says, "I have fought the good fight, I have finished the race, I have kept the faith. Finally, there is laid up for me the crown of righteousness, which the Lord, the righteous Judge, will give to me on that Day."[595] He did not say, "I have received the righteousness of God and the righteousness of Christ the day I believed," but the

---

593 Or: striving.
594 1 Corinthians 9:27.
595 2 Timothy 4:7–8.

crown of righteousness he will be given on that Day, on the Last Day.

But through his life and struggle, he says, "I press on, that I may lay hold of that for which Christ Jesus has also laid hold of me. Brethren, I do not count myself to have apprehended; but one thing I do, forgetting those things which are behind and reaching forward to those things which are ahead, I press toward the goal."[596] I quote these words, to remind, through them, those who say that they have ascended to the heavens with Christ and have sat down at the right hand of the Majesty on high, and through them also to remind those who proclaim the deification of man.

For St. Paul, after the aforementioned words, says, "Therefore let us, as many as are mature, have this mind."[597] And not only does he call the believers to press on, but also says, "Run in such a way that you may obtain it. And everyone who competes for the prize is temperate in all things."[598] Do we say to him, "Sorry, O great Saint, what need there be that we run and struggle and be temperate? Have we not received the free righteousness as a gift from God, according to explanation of your epistle to the Galatians?"

He who has ears to hear, let him hear!

13. Was the faith of our father Abraham without works?

Here we are faced with a question concerning our father Abraham: Was the faith of our father Abraham without works? Perhaps the calling came to him freely[599]—that is, if we do not speak in detail about his prior readiness of heart, which made him leave his people, his family, and his father's house, and as soon as he was called, he obeyed, so he departed, not knowing where he was going.[600]

But the author says, "And so was the faith of Abraham in God without works whatsoever," and, "Therefore, God began

---

596 Philippians 3:12–14.
597 Philippians 3:15.
598 1 Corinthians 9:24–25.
599 See Genesis 12:1–3.
600 See Hebrews 11:8.

the covenant with Abraham with no prior commandments and conditions, as it were with all humankind in him, freely." The author concludes from this, saying, "Here lies sin, that man trusts in his activity and the work of his hands in completing bodily commandments, above God's gift granted through faith freely, with no work or bodily activity with respect to man," and the author continues, saying, "God repeated the covenant with Abraham freely, without any prior work."

How can this be? The Scriptures speak to us about how our father Abraham, since the beginning of his calling, did not abandon the altar, wherever he moved[601], as a proof of his service of God; neither did he abandon the tent, as a proof of the life as a sojourner which he lived; nor did he abandon asceticism, by which he left for Lot the land more abundant in grass and wealth, taking for himself that which Lot left[602]; nor did the life obedience leave him at all, with which he took his only son to offer him [as] a whole burnt offering to God[603].

Do we deny all these virtues, and strip Abraham the patriarch of all his works? As for the calling which came to him freely, we place before it the saying of St. Paul the Apostle, concerning the Lord and those called according to His purpose: "For whom He foreknew, He also predestined.... Moreover, whom He predestined, these He also called."[604] God knew the heart of Abraham before He chose him and called him; therefore, there is no point to say about the covenant between God and Abraham that "this is the free covenant which is based on faith in God, without works or commandments."

The author also says in his explanation of the epistle to the Galatians, "Abraham lived by faith with God. So, when the Law went in unto his children, faith ceased and its blessings, and the works of the Law began for teaching, with its curses." The Law was given through Moses the prophet, who is one of the children of Abraham. So did faith cease in the days of Moses, with all the

---

601 See Genesis 12.
602 See Genesis 13.
603 See Genesis 22.
604 Romans 8:29–30.

miracles which God did through his hands? Or was there not the deepest faith which split the Red Sea, and the people passing through it on dry land[605]? Likewise, the faith by which the people were sustained on manna and quails for forty years, "that He might make you know that man shall not live by bread alone; but man lives by every word that proceeds from the mouth of the LORD."[606] And throughout these forty years, their garments did not wear out on them, nor did their feet swell.[607] So, did faith cease in the days of the Law of Moses? And did it cease in the days of Joshua and the long chain of the prophets? And did the curses settle on [them] with the works of the Law, as the author says? Or were not blessings pronounced too, with the curses? They were together, from Mount Gerizim for blessings, and from Mount Ebal for curses.[608] And how abundant the blessings are, which were mentioned in Deuteronomy 28:1–14.

It is known that curses began thousands of years before the Law, such as the curse of Cain[609] and the curse of the flood which destroyed the people[610]. The Law is not always linked to the curse, as the author sees. But sin is linked to the curse. And sin was known, with its punishments, before the Law of Moses, when the conscience took the place of the law, with its judgments, and we call it "the natural law" or "the moral, unwritten law."

After all that we have said, we would like to ask the following important question regarding works.

14. What is the point of works, their necessity and their significance?

Works are the fruit of faith, signifying that it is a living faith. The Scripture says, "Every tree which does not bear good fruit is

---

605 "On dry land" is literally "within it."
606 Deuteronomy 8:3.
607 See Deuteronomy 8:4.
608 See Deuteronomy 27:12–13.
609 See Genesis 4:11.
610 See Genesis 6.

cut down and thrown into the fire."[611] The fruits are the works. The Lord says regarding this, "By their fruits you will know them,"[612] and likewise does our teacher St. James the Apostle say, "And I will show you my faith by my works."[613]

Works are the evidence of responding to the work of grace and of the fellowship with the Holy Spirit. For grace works in man but does not force him to do good. Man however must do good by his free will. Works then are the evidence that man is responding to the work of grace, and evidence that when the Spirit of God worked in us, we partnered with Him. We did not quench the Spirit[614], did not resist the Spirit[615], and did not grieve the Spirit[616]. But, by our works, we have entered into the communion of the Holy Spirit, according to the teaching of the Scripture[617] and according to the blessing of the Church.

Works are a proof of our obedience to the commandments of God. The Master Lord says, "Whoever hears these sayings of Mine, and does them, I will liken him to a wise man who built his house on the rock,"[618] and He also says, "Whoever does and teaches them [the commandments], he shall be called great in the kingdom of heaven."[619]

15. What are the limits of "through us," "in us," and "with Him"?

The author's problem is that, instead of believing that the Lord Christ took[620] a human body, he sees that He took the body of our humanity, meaning the body of all men. Therefore, he sees that

---

611 Matthew 3:10. Also see Matthew 7:19.
612 Matthew 7:20.
613 James 2:18.
614 See 1 Thessalonians 5:19.
615 See Acts 7:51.
616 See Ephesians 4:30.
617 See 2 Corinthians 13:14.
618 Matthew 7:24.
619 Matthew 5:19.
620 "Took" is literally "was incarnate in."

when He died on the cross, He died through us or in us, or all humankind died with Him. And so, when He arose from the dead, He arose in us [i.e. in our body] and we arose with Him, and so, in his opinion, we died through the death of the Lord Christ, and arose through His resurrection. And he goes further to say that we descended into Hades, ascended with Him into the heavens, entered the Holies above, and sat down at the right hand of the Majesty. All these ideas are clear in his book on Paul the Apostle, and in his interpretation of the epistle to the Romans and his interpretation of the epistle to the Galatians, which we are presently addressing.

16. Did we descend with Him into Hades, and did we pay the judgment of death?

The author says in his explanation of the epistle to the Galatians:

> For we died with Christ and arose with Him. For He died through us and arose through us. By the power of death, we descended into Hades[621] and completed the maximum punishment and judgment which were imposed on us as sinners and transgressors. And by the power of the resurrection, we ascended and rose up from Hades and the pit—but from the earth itself—to[622] God, that we may live with Him in Christ.

We would like to mention two remarks on his words:

1. Did we die with Christ on the cross and arose with Him from the pit? Or were our death and resurrection with Him in Baptism, according to the teaching of Paul the Apostle himself, as it came in the epistle to the Romans, "Or do you not know that as many of us as were baptized into Christ Jesus were baptized into His death? Therefore, we were buried with Him through baptism into death.... For if we have been united together in the likeness of His death, certainly we also shall be in the likeness of His

---

621 Literally: the pit.
622 Arabic text adds here: the domain of.

resurrection."[623] And as it came also in the epistle to the Colossians, "Buried with Him in baptism, in which you also were raised with Him."[624]

So, did we die twice with Him, once on the cross and the second in Baptism? What is the point of dying with Him in Baptism if we have died with Him on the cross?

As for our descending with Him into Hades[625], no one has said this before, and it has no theological purpose. Christ descended into Hades to take from it those who have reposed in the faith and to transfer them to paradise. So what is the point that we descend with Him into Hades?

2. As for "we descended into Hades and completed the maximum punishment and judgment which were imposed on us as sinners and transgressors," this is completely against the doctrine of redemption. We did not pay the judgment of death imposed on us, but Christ paid it on our behalf. We did not die for our sins, otherwise there would not be redemption. Redemption means that Christ died for us—instead of us—and saved us from death, and on this the Scripture says, "But God demonstrates His own love toward us, in that while we were still sinners, Christ died for us.... For if when we were enemies we were reconciled to God through the death of His Son."[626]

Therefore, if we were the ones who died, descended into Hades and completed the maximum punishment and judgment which were imposed on us—as the author says—then there would not be redemption there. As long as we died and completed the maximum punishment and judgment which were imposed on us as sinners and transgressors, why then did Christ die? And what is the meaning of "died for us"? What is then the author's understanding of redemption? And what is the meaning of the saying of the Scripture about the Lord Christ, "But He was wounded for our

---

623 Romans 6:3–5.
624 Colossians 2:12.
625 Literally: the pit.
626 Romans 5:8, 10.

transgressions, He was bruised for our iniquities"[627]?

17. Did we die the eternal death?

The author says in his explanation of the epistle to the Galatians:

> He who has died has become innocent of sin. Why? Because he has paid God's sentence[628] on the sinner to eternal death. And **we have died not with the ordinary bodily death, but with the eternal death**. And it is impossible for man to obtain this except through the death of Christ. For Christ died for the sake of our sins. And **we have died with Him for the sake of our sins**… for our death with Christ established for us the fulfillment of the sentence[629] of eternal death. And by this, we have become innocent of the judgment, and consequently we have become innocent of our sins… And so we have become innocent for good of sin as a deadly act. So, sin no longer has authority; neither does the one, who has authority to make [people] fall into sin, have authority over us.

The time for eternal death is not in this world, but after the general Judgment, as the Scripture says regarding the Day of Judgment, "And these will go away into everlasting punishment, but the righteous into eternal life."[630] The sound expression is that we did not die the eternal death, but we have escaped eternal death through the death of Christ on our behalf. And we say likewise regarding the statement "We become innocent of sin" and "We have received exoneration" which have appeared repeatedly in the writings of the author. We have not become innocent of sin, but have received pardon from the punishment of sin. The innocent is the one who has not committed a sin, and "We have received exoneration" means we have become innocent. Yet we are not innocent, but sinners, and we are under sentence. We have, however,

---

627   Isaiah 53:5.
628   Or: judgment.
629   Ibid.
630   Matthew 25:46.

received a pardon or immunity from the sentence pronounced against us, in that Christ bore it in our place.

18. Are we more than victorious and sin has no authority over us?

The author says in his explanation of the epistle to the Galatians:

> For the power of our death has become working in us spiritually, in an unceasing and eternal way. Therefore, with it we have overcome all the power of evil in the world. For the power of the death of Christ, in which we have shared, released us of every sin and every blame. So the devil or any evil power has no longer access in us. For the power of our resurrection has become working in us spiritually, in an unceasing and eternal way. Therefore, it made us more than victorious. For it took us once and for all out of the sphere of conflict with the enemy, having placed us in the sphere of God in Christ.

Do these words [reflect] the reality in our practical life? Do we not sin daily? St. John the Apostle says, "If we say that we have no sin, we deceive ourselves, and the truth is not in us."[631] Also, in the prayer for the departed, we say, "For no one is without sin, even though his life on earth be a single day." What is the meaning of "it took us once and for all out of the sphere of conflict with the enemy," as the author says, while St. Peter the Apostle says, "Be sober, be vigilant; because your adversary the devil walks about like a roaring lion, seeking whom he may devour. Resist him, steadfast in the faith."[632] And St. Paul the Apostle reproves the Hebrews, saying, "You have not yet resisted to bloodshed, striving against sin."[633] So how does the author say, "it took us once and for all out of the sphere of conflict with the enemy"?

---

631 1 John 1:8.
632 1 Peter 5:8–9.
633 Hebrews 12:4.

19. Have we become then without sin before the Law?

The author says in his explanation of the epistle to the Galatians, "The Son of God died, bearing the sins of man. And so the authority of the Law ceased forever, that man may live without sin, in the faith of Christ."

He also says in his explanation of the epistle to the Romans, "For the Christian stands before the Law without sin, having no sin against him. And here too the authority of the Law ceases and forever," and says, "The connection between Christians and the Law is cut off, and it no longer has cases raised against any person."

More alarming, however, than all this is that he says in his explanation of the epistle to the Galatians:

> Can the Christian person after that say, "I am a sinner"? But I will borrow the saying of St. Paul and say, "I do not set aside the grace of God." For if sin were stronger than the death of Christ, you judge. I have died with Christ [as] a price for my sins, so the life I now live, I live in the righteousness of Christ!

No, there is not a man in existence who has died [as] a price for his sins. Rather, Christ died for our sins, all of us.

As for the author's question, "Can the Christian person after that say, 'I am a sinner'?" the answer is that the Lord Christ has taught us to say daily in the Lord's prayer, "And forgive us our sins, for we also forgive."[634] And the holy Church teaches us to pray in the litanies of the Twelfth Hour [of the Agpeya], "Behold, I am about to stand before the just judge terrified and trembling because of my many sins." Also the priest, before beginning the Divine Liturgy, makes a prostration before the congregation and says, "I have sinned; forgive me." Monks, too, in their gathering for prayer, say to each other, "I have sinned; forgive me," or, "I have sinned; absolve me." Here we would like to repeat the author's question, "Can the Christian person after that say, 'I am a sinner'?"

---

634 Luke 11:4.

The Lord Christ justified the tax collector who said, "God, be merciful to me a sinner!"[635] but did not justify the Pharisee who spoke of his own righteousness before God.[636]

20. What about then the rebellion of the body and its lusts?

Along with the author's saying that sin has no authority over the Christian person, he goes back to mention the rebellion of the body and its lusts, saying in his explanation of the epistle to the Galatians, "Man, however, remains, even with the help of the Holy Spirit and grace, under the pressure and importunity of the body and its lusts. But he feels, despite the rebellion of the body, that he is victorious through grace. And the offenses of the body do not abolish the work of grace in all the domains of the spirit," and he says, "Yes, the body may be harmed, but the spirit and soul are not touched. For we, through the body and in the body, may be found defeated, because the body is fallen under the powers of the world and time. But in the spirit, we are more than victorious."

We are astonished at this contradiction: How are we overcome in the body, but in the spirit, we are more than victorious? And [the contradiction] between the rebellion of the body and victory of the spirit.

The author says in his explanation of the epistle to the Galatians:

My reader, you who are suffering from the body and its lusts, there is no salvation except by grace. Know perfectly well **that your past and future sins Christ bore** in His body on the cross. For they do not exist with God, but in your own conscience which the devil torments with illusions, to pressure you by despair. There is no sin against you with Christ, but unto you there is grace with Christ.

We note that he says "there is no salvation except by grace," while Paul the Apostle says, "You have not yet resisted to bloodshed,

---
635 Luke 18:13.
636 See Luke 18:11–12.

striving against sin,"⁶³⁷ and St. Peter says, "Resist him, steadfast in the faith."⁶³⁸ And he says to this man who is suffering from the lusts of the body, "There is no sin against you with Christ, but unto you there is grace with Christ." This subject requires to be addressed when discussing his book which is about this subject.

21. Did we ascend with Christ and entered God's Holies above?

The author says in one of his books, "St. Paul accumulates the justifications which we need that we may have the boldness and confidence in our ascension with Christ, and our entrance with Christ God's Holies above itself. For he places in our hands the same qualification which was in the hands of Christ, and which qualified Him to enter the Holies." And he says, "This St. Paul considers a personal qualification which we need to share in the ascension of the Lord and His entrance, as a right of our core rights," and he says, "Where Christ is now, we have the right to be [there]."

Truly an astonishing boldness, that men are made equal with Christ. And he says, "in our hands the same qualification which was in the hands of Christ," and it is one of our rights, that we be where Christ is. I do not desire to comment on these words now; I fear what I would say.

"He who justifies the wicked, and he who condemns the just, both of them alike are an abomination to the Lord."⁶³⁹

---

637 Hebrews 12:4.
638 1 Peter 5:9.
639 Proverbs 17:15.

CHAPTER TWELVE

The Deification of Man

Introduction

Had the deification of man, with its details, been a slip of the pen or a slip of the thought, I would not have given it such a high degree of care. But the subject is spreading in many of the author's books, and his disciples are defending it to death. Had it merely been a matter of disciples defending their teacher, I would have excused them for their love for him, but the matter goes beyond that, in that they are trying to prove that this subject of deification is [of] the thought of the Fathers and the heritage of the saints, and that they are [only] repeating the understanding of the Fathers. Therefore, I saw that necessity is prompting me to explain this matter.

1. The matter of deification is the angel's first sin.

The desire to deification is the first fall for the free, rational beings. The devil was an angel of the host of the cherubim.[640] The Lord said of him, "You were the seal of perfection, full of wisdom and perfect in beauty."[641] He was perfect in his ways, from the day he was created till iniquity was found in him[642]. So how did this

---

640 See Ezekiel 28:14, 16.
641 Ezekiel 28:12.
642 See Ezekiel 28:15.

"anointed cherub who covers"[643] fall? And how was iniquity found in him? This is explained in the book of Isaiah, saying, "For you have said in your heart: 'I will ascend into heaven, I will exalt my throne above the stars of God.... I will ascend above the heights of the clouds, I will be like the Most High.' Yet you shall be brought down to Sheol, to the lowest depths of the Pit."[644]

2. With the same desire to being a god, the devil enticed the first man.

For he said to Eve, "You will be like God, knowing good and evil."[645] And so, man, having desired the glory of the Divinity—and though [desiring only] a single attribute of It—lost therefore the glory of the humanity which was his. And as an evolution of the desire to being a god, came polytheism, the tales of the Pagan gods, and the worship of kings and Pharaohs.

3. "You shall have no other gods before Me."[646]

This was a divine warning of this fall, God having alerted to it in the first of the ten commandments. Man being a god himself is undoubtedly more grievous than he having other gods!

4. Of the gravity of deification, we mention the tragedy of King Herod.

He did not say that he was a god; neither was it mentioned that he desired that. But when he gave an oration to the people, decked in his majestic kingly garment, the people shouting, "The voice of a god and not of a man!"[647] Herod did not rebuke them, and as though he accepted these words from them. "Then immediately an angel of the Lord struck him, because he did not give glory to

---

643 Ezekiel 28:14.
644 Isaiah 14:13–15.
645 Genesis 3:5.
646 Exodus 20:3.
647 Acts 12:22.

God. And he was eaten by worms and died."[648] To this extent did the gravity of the deification of man reach.

5. The deification of man means to be characterized by Divine attributes.

For man to become a god means that he becomes infinite, filling the heavens and the earth, that he be a searcher of the hearts and thoughts, who knows the sins [of others], who exists everywhere, who is a performer of miracles by his own power! The meaning of being a god is that he is holy, infallible. The deification of man denies that he is a created being, but an eternal god who has no beginning. And man being a god means that he does not die! So, who dares ascribe to man all these attributes?

6. Therefore, it is impossible that one of the [Church] Fathers has proclaimed this deification.

If an author, whoever he may be, makes such a claim, it is either that he did not understand what that saintly [Church] Father said; or that there may be a mistake in the translation of the saying of the [Church] Father from Greek, of whose knowledge these brethren boast; or that there may be an attempt to hide behind the Fathers, by ascribing to the Fathers that which they did not say or that which they did not mean. And this [latter] is another mistake.

I marvel to the uttermost when I read in the writings of those who call for the deification of man phrases [like] "All the Fathers say," "the summary of the teaching of the Fathers," or, "the Fathers' interpretation of this point." So have you read all the sayings of the Fathers and all their interpretations? And it is known that understanding the mind [or thought] of a particular saint is not only [knowing] a statement he said—or was ascribed to him—on a particular occasion, but it is a study of the mind [or thought] of that saint in all his writings.

It may happen that one of the theologians specializes solely in

---
648 Acts 12:23.

the sayings of one of the Fathers, or that a Ph.D. candidate may study a single book by one of the Fathers. So how does one dare say in his discourse the phrase "All the Fathers say," "the summary of the teaching of the Fathers," or, "the Fathers' interpretation"? The one who respects precision in his manner [of writing] must rise above such boldness, especially when he is dealing with theological subjects.

Those who call for the deification of man consider that whoever does not accept deification is "under the dominion of biological birth,"—that is, the bodily birth and not the birth from above—and that "he perhaps refrains [from accepting it] out of faintheartedness or feeling unworthy of the grace of Christ, this if he were of a simple, good intent."

Numerous erroneous teachings

In addition to their usage of the word "deification" and its derivatives, there are many other phrases that lead to the same meaning, of which we mention the following.

7. They proclaim a union between a Divine nature and a human nature!

This is what the author says in his book. What is theologically known is that the only one in whom the Divine nature was united with human nature was the Lord Christ—to whom be glory—in His Incarnation. So, did the Apostles become fully like Him on the day of Pentecost when the Holy Spirit came upon them? The author says about the day of Pentecost:

> Then we are [standing] before a "bush burning with fire," according to the symbol; or a Divine nature united with a human nature, according to the explanation of the symbol; or the image of the prophecy of the Nativity of Christ, as we have received [it] from Holy Tradition.

No, we have not received from Holy Tradition the occurrence

of a union [between] a Divine nature and human nature in the Apostles when the Holy Spirit came upon them on the day of Pentecost.

Attacking the Divinity of Christ is [accomplished] in one of two ways: either the lowering of the Lord Christ to the level of men, as the Arians did; or, the lifting up of men to the level of Christ, as those say who proclaim the deification of man; or, as it is said concerning the day of Pentecost, that a union took place in the disciples between a Divine nature and a human nature. And thus, there would be no difference between men and Christ. And the Divine Incarnation would not be the only miracle [of its kind], in that it belonged [solely] to the Lord Christ, but the Apostles resemble Him in this, and consequently the whole Church.

8. "The purpose of the Divine Incarnation reached its pinnacle on the day of Pentecost."

So does the author say in his book, and he explains this by saying, "What was started in Bethlehem happened and was completed in the upper room."

He means that what was started in Bethlehem, regarding the Divine Incarnation, is the union between the Divine nature and the human nature in the Person of the Lord Christ. And this same situation was completed in the upper room on the day of Pentecost. And thus the purpose of the Divine Incarnation reached its pinnacle! As it appeared in another place in this same book, he improperly quoted [St. Augustine], "Marvel, be glad, we are made Christ."[649]

9. The Church is a human nature united with a Divine nature!

So says the author in his book, "Christ united with the Church, so the Church acquired all that belongs to Christ." The phrase "all that belongs to Christ" here carries a clear theological error. For

---

649 Augustine *Homilies on the Gospel of John* XXI.V(20–23).8 (NPNF¹ 7:140).

Christ has Divinity which the Church did not acquire. Christ has a relationship with the Father, of which He says, "I and My Father are one,"[650] and this relationship the Church did not acquire. Christ is characterized by being infinite with respect to time, space, and power. And this also the Church did not acquire. How dangerous is the use of the word "all" in theological expressions. It must not be used except with precision and caution.

I have notified [the author] of the mistakes which came in his book many years ago. Nevertheless, the book was reprinted exactly as is in 1981, then a third time in 2002. Also, the same mistakes were repeated in 1978 and 1988 in the last page of his book on the Incarnation. And finally, the disciples of the author published a book in defense of him, which they titled *The Church, the Bride of Christ: A Human Nature United with a Divine Nature.* This [latter] book is an adherence to the same mistake and insistence on it. Perhaps he desires to take the readers back to what resembles the heresy of Pantheism. So all are a single being which is a Divine nature united with a human nature! Through the will of God, we will respond to what was written in this [book] and what came in other books by the author concerning this subject.

Also in the author's book on the Incarnation, we see the same insistence on this idea, for he says concerning the Church and the Divine Incarnation, that the Church is an extension of the Divine Incarnation.

10. The Church is an extension of the Divine Incarnation.

He says, "The Church is an extension of the Divine Incarnation, that is, of the mystery of Christ," and, "She becomes an extension of the indescribable, hypostatic oneness which Christ made between His Divinity and His humanity in the depth of His being, since [the time of] His conception." He also says, "The truth of the Church, which is His divine body, where the being of the Church itself springs from the being of the body of Christ." He took this

---

650 John 10:30.

last phrase from the French scholar, Fr. Du Manoir.[651] The author also says, "The Church is considered an extension of the immense divine body which fills heaven and earth. And the mystery of the Church is considered an extension of the indescribable mystery of the Divine Incarnation, that is, the mystery of the union of the Divinity with the humanity in Christ."

This is a huge confusion between the Church—which is the congregation of the believers, which was considered the bride of Christ and His body[652]—and the body of Christ, which was born of the Virgin, with which the Divinity united in the womb of the Virgin.

The author says that through the Holy Spirit, whom the disciples received on the day of Pentecost, "they all became, in this new fullness, partakers in the Divine nature," and he continues, saying, "And so, the Church is shown to be fundamentally raised upon the partnership in the Divine nature through the Holy Spirit. And by that she is shown in the depth of her being, that she is a unity between the Divinity and humanity through the Holy Spirit, as an extension of the hypostatic unity which was accomplished in Christ."

Who can accept these words, theologically? And who accepts spreading it among men? Who accepts that the Church, which is the congregation of the believers, is an extension of the hypostatic unity between the Divinity and humanity? Is the Church united with the Divinity as an extension of the Divine Incarnation? And does the author call for the deification of the Church? This reminds us of another phrase in one of the author's books, which is as follows.

11. The Apostles [who are men] were united with the Holy Spirit as a hypostasis.

The author repeats this again in another book of his.

---

651   See H. Du Manoir, *Dogme et Spiritualité chez S. Cyrille d'Alexandrie*. (Paris: Librairie Philosophique Vrin, 1944).
652   See Ephesians 5.

As long as the Holy Spirit is the Spirit of God, uniting with the Holy Spirit as a hypostasis is a kind of deification or Divine Incarnation—and this is a known heresy. If man were united hypostatically with the Spirit of God, he then never sins, and it would not be said of him that he grieves the Spirit[653] nor that he quenches the Spirit[654]. Nor would he be subject to the saying of the Apostle: "If anyone defiles the temple of God, God will destroy him."[655] For how can he defile the temple of God while he is united with the Holy Spirit hypostatically? This hypostatic dwelling undoubtedly results in infallibility.

The dwelling of the Holy Spirit is the dwelling of grace and not dwelling hypostatically. Thus, we pray in the [absolution of the] Third Hour of the Agpeya, and say to the Lord,

> We thank You for You raised us for prayer in this holy hour, in which You abundantly poured the grace of Your Holy Spirit upon Your holy disciples and honorable and blessed apostles, like tongues of fire.... Send forth upon us the grace of Your Holy Spirit, and purify us from all defilement of body and spirit.

We never use the phrase "the Hypostasis of the Holy Spirit," but His grace.

The grace of the Holy Spirit which we receive does not deprive us of the grace of freedom. We are free to accept the work of the Holy Spirit in us and participate with the Spirit in the work, so we enter into the communion of the Holy Spirit. Likewise, we are free to resist the Spirit, or grieve the Spirit, or quench the Spirit. And then it is necessary for us to say to the Lord concerning Him, "Do not take Him away from us, O Good One, but we ask You to renew Him within us,"[656] and we say to the Holy Spirit, "Graciously come, and dwell in us."[657] Note that in all these we speak of "dwelling"

---

653 See Ephesians 4:30.
654 See 1 Thessalonians 5:19.
655 1 Corinthians 3:17.
656 Third Hour of Agpeya – Litanies.
657 Ibid.

and not "uniting." Also, in the epistle to the Corinthians, he speaks of "dwelling" and not "uniting."[658]

Those who claim the deification of man, after proclaiming the hypostatic dwelling of the Holy Spirit in man, advanced to speaking of the dwelling of Christ in us.

12. The hypostatic dwelling of Christ in man.

In one of his books, the author believes that Christ dwells hypostatically in man! In this book he says about the Lord Christ, "And we also live in Him with the selfsame divine fullness with the Father and the Son and the Holy Spirit. For where Christ dwells, [there] dwells the divine fullness." Astonishing and daring is this phrase "we live with the selfsame divine fullness."

The dwelling of Christ in us is not a hypostatic dwelling, nor with the selfsame divine fullness, but it is a dwelling through faith, according to the verse which is the title of his book, "that Christ may dwell in your hearts through faith."[659] The author, however, insists on the dwelling of Christ with the fullness of His Divinity in man. So he says in the aforementioned book, "It is true that the historical birthplace of Christ was a manger of mud, but spiritually, it is impossible that Christ dwells with the fullness of His Divinity except in man. This is His message for the sake of which He came down from heaven." "With the fullness of His Divinity … in man"? How shocking!

He says, "It is impossible that Christ dwells with the fullness of His Divinity except in man." This makes one wonder, for He dwells with the fullness of His Divinity everywhere—in heaven and on earth. What does the word "impossible" here mean? And as a result of the dwelling of Christ with the fullness of His Divinity, the matter goes into the Mystery of the Eucharist, and here we ask, regarding their belief in this Mystery: "Do we eat and drink the Divinity in the Mystery of the Eucharist?"

---

658 See 1 Corinthians 3:16.
659 Ephesians 3:17.

13. Do we eat and drink the Divinity in the Mystery of the Eucharist?

The answer is evident in their book, for they say, "We drink the Divinity—of course, mystically—and we drink the life-giving Blood, according to grace and not according to a bodily standard."

We answer, saying that the Lord Christ said, "Whoever eats My flesh and drinks My blood,"[660] and did not say, "Whoever eats and drinks My Divinity." God is Spirit,[661] and the Spirit is not eaten nor drunk.

Likewise, the one who eats the Divine nature, and It abides in him, comes out of Communion a God, whom those [present] in Church worship. We, however, encounter a problem here, which is the following: What about those who partake of Communion in an unworthy manner? Does he eat the Divinity and drink the Divinity, and "eats and drinks judgment to himself"[662] at the same time?

14. What is the meaning of the phrase "I said, 'You are gods.'"

Those who proclaim the deification of man rely on an erroneous understanding of the Psalm, "I said, 'You are gods, and all of you are children of the Most High.'"[663] So let us study together the meaning of this statement.

The word "gods" here means lords or masters, and does not mean Divinity, as evidenced by his saying after it, "But you shall die like men, and fall like one of the princes."[664] For those who die and fall are not gods, because God is Holy, and He lives and does not die. Then "gods" here carries the meaning of masters or lords. And God is the Lord of lords[665], and Master of masters too.

---

660 John 6:54.
661 See John 4:24.
662 1 Corinthians 11:29.
663 Psalms 82:6.
664 Psalms 82:7.
665 See Revelation 19:16.

The word "god," with the meaning of master or lord, is used in many places in the Holy Scriptures, for example, the saying of the Lord to Moses the prophet, "See, I have made you as God to Pharaoh."[666] This does not at all mean that he [that is, Moses] is the creator of Pharaoh, but is merely his master. Likewise, the Lord said to Moses, when he excused himself from this mission with the excuse that he was not eloquent, "Is not Aaron the Levite your brother? I know that he can speak well…. And I will be with your mouth and with his mouth…. So he shall be your spokesman to the people. And he himself shall be as a mouth for you, and you shall be to him as God."[667] What is meant by "you shall be to him as God" is that "you shall give him the inspiration of what he says," and not that "you shall be to him a Creator." For Aaron was born before Moses.

Those who proclaim the divinity of man have no reason, then, to use this verse in their book. Sadly, they include the statement, "And we are made like Him according to the richness of His goodness, and we shall be gods and sons of God." And they attribute this erroneous understanding to one of the Fathers.

15. What is the meaning of the Apostle's saying "We shall be like Him"[668]?

We need to show the meaning of the phrase "like Him." St. John the Apostle was talking about the Second Coming of Christ and about being like Him in the Other World, with glorified bodies as St. Paul the Apostle said in his epistle to the Philippians concerning the Lord Christ, "who will transform our lowly body that it may be conformed to His glorious body, according to the working by which He is able…"[669] and as he also said to the Corinthians[670].

And so St. John said, "Beloved, now we are children of God;

---

666 Exodus 7:1.
667 Exodus 4:14–16.
668 1 John 3:2.
669 Philippians 3:21.
670 See 1 Corinthians 15:44.

and it has not yet been revealed what we shall be, but we know that when He is revealed, we shall be like Him, for we shall see Him as He is. And everyone who has this hope in Him purifies himself."[671] He is not saying that we are like Him in the Divine nature, but concerning our state at the appearance of the Lord in the Second Coming. Nevertheless, he says, "It has not yet been revealed what we shall be."

Those proclaiming the deification of man, however, hold onto the word "like" and use it to mean something other than its meaning, and in a different place than its own. So they say in their book: "The Lord was born of the Virgin in Bethlehem for our sakes, and not for His sake, and became as one of us that we may become like Him." And they say in the same book:

> That we will be like Christ, this is a firm hope based on a conclusive text that does not permit more than one interpretation. But it does not say in equality. For the word "like" in the New Testament especially means the fellowship in the selfsame nature and does not mean equality.

And they include some biblical examples that have nothing to do with the deification of man. Nevertheless, they speak of this equality in many places. They continue this subject, saying:

> Behind this use lies the truth of man's creation in the image of God and according to His likeness (Genesis 1:26). Then Christ came to renew our dead, corrupt image, and restore it to its high position. And if this hope is lost from us, by what form or likeness do we purify ourselves, and what is the biological power in the whole earth and heaven itself, which turn man to the glorious, victorious image of Christ, except the fellowship in the origin in God who made us according to His likeness.

When God created us in His image and according to His

---

[671] 1 John 3:2–3.

likeness, He did not create us in His nature. And had He created us in His nature, it would have been impossible for man to fall. He created us, however, in His image: in purity, in authority, in freedom of will, in intellect, and the like. And our restoration to our original image does not mean restoration to deification nor to the fellowship in the origin in God, as they say.

16. What is the meaning of, "He took what is ours, and gave us what is His"?

This is a phrase quoted from the Midnight Praises [Friday Theotokia], which they repeat more than once in their book as though this were a proof of the deification of man which they rely upon.

God did not give us what is His with respect to the Divinity, absolutely not. He gave us righteousness, sonship, authority to bind and loose in the Priesthood[672], and gave us—or to some of us—the power to perform miracles, not through our nature but through His name, as St. Peter the Apostle said in the healing of the paralytic at the Beautiful Gate.[673]

He did not, however, give us what is His concerning the Divinity. Otherwise we would not have sinned and would not have died, and would have become infinite. In the same way one should understand the phrase "He took what is ours," for He did not take everything, but "resembled us in everything, except for sin alone."[674] In theological matters, meticulousness is required, and one should not take a phrase with its absolute meaning, but within its limits and its connotation.

17. "The glory which You gave Me I have given them."[675]

---

672 See Matthew 18:18 and John 20:22–23.
673 See Acts 3:12, 16.
674 The Divine Liturgy According to St. Gregory – Prayer of Reconciliation.
675 John 17:22.

In the same manner, we will address here the saying of the Lord concerning His disciples: "The glory which You gave Me I have given them."[676] The glory of the Lord Christ is infinite, and He did not give to the disciples all His glory. He did not give to them the glory of the Divinity, for this is impossible and it is contrary to the saying of the Lord in the Book of Isaiah: "My glory I will not give to another."[677]

They took many glories concerning the gifts and authority, within the limits which their human nature can endure. And all that He gave to them is a human, spiritual glory. There is no reason then for the author to include this verse in his book, and there is no reason for his disciples to include it, in their attempt to speak of the deification of man.

We would like to reiterate here what we previously said that not every word is to be taken with its absolute meaning, and that the word "all" must not be used in theological expression without meticulousness. As the author said in one of his books, which he repeated at the end of another book of his, "Christ united with the Church, so the Church acquired all that belongs to Christ." The Church did not acquire all that belongs to Christ. She did not acquire His Divinity, nor His oneness with the Father[678].

18. Does the Holy Spirit fashion us in the nature of the Son of God?

The author says about Baptism in one of his books, "After the Holy Spirit begets us in Baptism and fashions us in the nature of the Son of God, He cannot but bear witness to our spirits that we are sons of God."

The nature of the Son of God is Divinity united with humanity. And this matter we do not acquire at all in Baptism. Therefore, it is impossible that the Holy Spirit fashions us in the nature of the Son of God. Rather, we are born of water and the Spirit, and we are

---

676 John 17:22.
677 Isaiah 42:8.
678 See John 10:30.

called sons of God in another meaning; therefore, it was said of the Lord Christ that He is the only begotten Son[679].

The nature of the Son of God—that He is a Son of the essence of God and His Divinity, through an eternal sonship. As for us, we have sonship through faith[680], through love, or through adoption[681].

19. Is God not "an another" with respect to man?

The author says in one of his books, "A person, when he speaks, informs us about himself from a distance through words, or gives us information, help, or knowledge. And this person remains distant from our being. And after he speaks to us, he remains as 'an another.' But God, when He spoke, spoke so that by the word He may enter our life, and become as a Self in self..." Then he says, "God here, after speaking, did not become an another with respect to man. Having become God to man means that He has become closer to man than everything else, but has become as the soul of man and his self! And based on this law itself, God in the Holy Scriptures did not speak at all except to prove this truth, deepen it, and ensure its enforcement."

So if God were not "an another" with respect to man, would God and man be a single being? And as the author says, "a Self in self."

20. Is Bethlehem the birthplace of humanity?

The author says in his book, that the Church is the bride of Christ and is His body which He took of the Virgin, "So He was born united with her with His Divinity. That is, the Church was born united with Christ the day Christ was born. And consequently, every one of us was born in Bethlehem, so it became the birthplace of the redeemed humanity."

It makes one wonder that he says that the Church was born of

---

679 See John 3:16, 18 and John 1:18.
680 See John 1:12.
681 See Romans 8:15, 22.

the Virgin the day Christ was born, and that the Church was born united with the Divinity!

And here the reader is left drowning in question marks and exclamation points! Was the Church born of the Virgin the day Christ was born? Or was she born on the day of Pentecost of the Holy Spirit? Or is she born from Baptism, a member by member, each in his day? Or has the birth of all the members of the Church not been accomplished yet? For there are people who will be born and baptized, and there are others who will join the faith in the future and join the membership of the Church.

What is the meaning of the Church was born united with the Divinity? Is she also equal to Christ, [being] of two natures, Divine and human, united?

And what causes one to wonder is that these words of the author, which came in his book, his disciples defended with all their might in a book, in the chapter titled "The Birthplace of the Redeemed Humanity," defending what their teacher wrote in his book. They defend the same opinion, trying to prove it through sayings from Midnight Praises, writings of the Fathers, or through "the mystical union," as they say, using quotes that have nothing to do with the subject. This shows us the danger of spreading a particular teaching of a teacher through his disciples. We perhaps need to return to this subject and the errors of their book in details.

He says about the Apostles on the day of Pentecost, "that an invisible union took place between a Divine nature and a human nature." And they [his disciples] have published a book titled "The Church, the bride of Christ: a human nature united with a Divine nature."

21. Are we clothed with the Divinity, within and without?

This was said concerning likening the Virgin Mary during the holy pregnancy, to the ark of the covenant that was overlaid with gold within and without, which contained the pot of manna which is a symbol of the Lord Christ. And so it was said, "You too, O Mary, are clothed with the glory of the Divinity, within and without,"[682] considering that the Word of God was within her, that the Holy Spirit came upon her for an embryo to be brought into being within her, and that the power of the Highest overshadowed her[683].

Those, however, who proclaim the deification of man say in their book, that "what was said about, and what came upon the Mother of God came upon the believers too." And they also say, "'The Holy Spirit filled every part of you, your soul and your body, O Mother of God,'[684] and this selfsame Spirit we, human beings, received because of the Virgin." And this is not surprising that those who said that they "acquired all that belongs to Christ," to say that they acquired all that belongs to the Virgin.

With respect to the equality with the Virgin, we ask them the following:

✣ Are you clothed with the Divinity, within and without?[685]

✣ Have you, as the Doxology for the Virgin says, become higher than the cherubim and the seraphim[686], and higher than the archangels?

✣ Are you standing at the right hand of the King, as it was said concerning the Virgin St. Mary, "At Your right hand stands the queen, O King"[687]?

✣ Has the Holy Spirit come upon you, and has the power of the Highest overshadow you?[688]

✣ Do all generations call you blessed?[689]

✣ Or have you become influenced by the Roman Catholic Church, in their reconsideration of the excessive magnification

---

682 Midnight Praises – Sunday Theotokia, Part 2.
683 See Luke 1:35.
684 See Midnight Praises – Saturday Watos Lobsh, the First Shiraat.
685 Midnight Praises – Sunday Theotokia, Part 2.
686 See Saturday Watos Psali for the Virgin Mary. (Translator's note).
687 See Psalms 45:9.
688 See Luke 1:35.
689 See Luke 1:48.

of the Virgin, as you say in the same book?

✣ Or have you become influenced by the Protestants of Plymouth who say that the Virgin is our sister?

My sons, do not err. Humble yourselves, repent, and reconsider what you are writing.

22. The position of man in Christ.

If you are speaking of man's position in Christ, of which you say that "with this we need to cry out in jubilation," know then that the way to reach the highest position is meekness [or gentleness] and humility, according to the teaching of Christ, "He who humbles himself will be exalted,"[690] and according to His saying, "Learn from Me, for I am gentle and lowly in heart."[691] And the position of man does not come through deification and exalting himself.

23. What is the meaning of "partakers of the Divine nature"[692]?

Finally, here is the most dangerous point, and I do not see that this article is sufficient for it; and this is: What is the meaning of "partakers of the Divine nature"?

Here we find that they twisted the verse in their publication. Where St. Peter the Apostle says, "partakers *of* the Divine nature," they say, "partakers *in* the Divine nature." And there is a vast difference between the two expressions. The expression "partakers of the Divine nature" means partakers with the nature, in the work, in the will, in building the kingdom of God. And this is not "partakers in the Divine nature," which means that we share in the nature of God.

Nevertheless, in their book, they repeat the expression "partakers in the Divine nature" twice in a page, and they say in

---

690 Matthew 23:12.
691 Matthew 11:29.
692 2 Peter 1:4.

the same page, "The expression 'eternal life' is another expression for the same truth, that is, fellowship[693] in the Divine nature." And as an explanation for the same expression, they say in the same book, "The Son came, was incarnate, died, and arose, that He may grant man steadfastness in not dying and immortality, through the fellowship [or sharing] in the Divinity."

How dare an author say concerning man "sharing in the Divinity." Nevertheless, they try to escape by saying, "likeness and not equality," as though the term "likeness" were light [and] acceptable. And they forget that the devil fell and perished because he used the word "like," and said in his heart, "I will be like the Most High."[694]

Receiving eternal life does not mean that we share in the nature of God. For although God is eternal, He is also infinite. For if man shared in the nature of God, he would become infinite like Him, and would also be omnipotent, existing everywhere, and searching the hearts and minds.

You must not take the word "eternity" and say that it is a proof for the fellowship in the Divine nature. Also, eternity is an inherent attribute of God, but, with respect to us, it is a reward or gift.

To prove the deification of man, they proclaim a strange expression: The deification of the humanity of the Lord Jesus. This is contrary to the uniting between the Divinity of the Lord and His humanity, where we say, "Without mingling, without confusion, and without alteration;" that is, the Divinity was not altered to become humanity, nor was the humanity altered to become Divinity. Otherwise, one of the natures would have vanished.

They, however, mention the expression "The deification of the humanity of the Lord Jesus" as a title in the same book, and this title is repeated several times. And they say, "And consequently, our fellowship in the incarnate Son does not become a fellowship in the humanity without the Divinity." They then claim a fellowship in the Divinity! And perhaps this is some of what our Muslim

---

693 Or: partaking or sharing.
694 Isaiah 14:14.

brethren call "polytheism."[695]

If all these [aforementioned] were strange, their dealing with the attribute of being from everlasting[696] is also strange. For they say in their book, "With perfect precision all the Fathers confirmed that the Son, who is from everlasting, turned our beginning or our origin to His divine Being." So, does our origin go back to God's Being? Have all the Fathers said this? Have they read all the writings of the Fathers, and seen in them this understanding? Is this not an encroachment on Patrology (Patristics)?

---

695 It means sharing in God, or having another God share in His Divinity.
696 Arabic: *azalia*.

CHAPTER THIRTEEN

Partakers of the Divine Nature

Introduction

Appending to that which we have said concerning the deification of man, we provide this supplement on partaking of the Divine nature. We will respond in this article to the thought, represented by a single school [of thought] as it appears in the book *St. Athanasius the Apostolic...* by Dr. George Habib Bibawy and a book by some of the monks of St. Macarius Monastery. And each of the two branches of this one school [of thought] translates the saying of St. Peter the Apostle, "partakers *of* the Divine nature,"[697] into "partakers *in* the Divine nature," meaning partakers in the selfsame Divine nature, and not partakers with the Divine nature, in the work and in the will, for example.

1. The expression "partakers in the Divine nature."

Dr. George Habib Bibawy mentions in his book *St. Athanasius the Apostolic...* the expression "partakers in the Divine nature" in the title of several chapters, and he uses "the partaking of the Eucharist as a partaking in the Divine nature," along with the [rest of the] details included under these titles.

He says, "The truth of our partaking in the Divinity because of our acquisition of this heavenly Mystery which grants eternal life,"

---

697 2 Peter 1:4 NKJV.

and he says, "That we may be able to partake in the Divinity of the Word." The audacity of this expression makes one marvel! And he also says, "The connection of the Incarnate Word with those whom He partook in their nature, that they partake in His Divinity."

In the book of the author's disciples, the following phrases are used: "the partaking in the Divine nature," "our partaking in God," "our partaking in the nature of the Trinity," and "the partaking in the nature of the Divinity."

It is impossible for us to accept the sharing with God in His nature and His Divinity, regardless of their attempt to justify this matter with meanings and quotations. So what do they say regarding this?

2. Did God desire our deification since [the time of] His creation of us?

They say that the deification of man is the divine purpose since the beginning. God's intention since the beginning was the deification of man, so when man sinned, this intention passed away.

These words are not acceptable, of course, for the following reasons:

✢ Had God's intention, since the beginning, been to deify man, He would not have created him capable of dying, in saying to him concerning the tree of the knowledge of good and evil, "For in the day that you eat of it you shall surely die."[698] That is, he is [created] with a nature capable of dying. And he truly died.

✢ Had God's intention, since the beginning, been the deification of man, He would have created him infallible, that is, incapable of falling into sin. Man was, however, prone to sin, and truly he did sin.

✢ Had God's intention been the deification of man, He would not have created him out of the dust and united with matter,

---

698 Genesis 2:17.

that is, with the body, while God is Spirit[699]. Then He was able to create him like the angels who are spirits[700]. And even those God created [as] spirits, some of them sinned.

And it is not an excuse to use the phrase "[You] blessed my nature in Yourself," which came in the Divine Liturgy according to St. Gregory. For blessing a nature is one thing, and deifying a nature is another. For God blessed our nature but did not deify it.

3. Did the Lord Christ deify His humanity?

Numerous are the phrases of the deification of the humanity and the deification of the body, in Dr. George Bibawy's book, for he says, "The resurrection of the body is the deification of the humanity;" "Christ deified His body after death;" "He deified the body and made this body immortal;" "the deification of the body of Christ is for this body to become immortal;" "the humanity which was deified by the union." He proclaims also that the lifting up of Christ, that is, His ascension, is the deification of His human nature.

It is evident that the Lord Christ took a body capable of dying, and He died.

As for the book of the author's disciples, they repeat the same idea [or thought] about the deification of the humanity of Christ, with many headings, saying, "The deification of the humanity of the Lord Jesus Christ."

We believe that the Divinity of Christ united with His humanity, without alteration. So, the Divinity did not become humanity, nor did the humanity become Divinity. Otherwise one of the natures would have vanished. So the humanity remained humanity and did not turn into Divinity. But it was glorified. And the Lord Christ arose by the power of His Divinity and ascended to the heavens by the power of His Divinity—and not because His humanity became Divinity! Rather, the humanity was glorified and

---

699 See John 4:24.
700 See Psalms 104:4.

was manifest in the resurrection and ascension.

And the dangerous thing is that, in proclaiming the deification of the body of Christ, they say that "the body which the Lord took from the Mother of God is our body."

4. Do we partake in the Divine nature through the adoption?

The following came in the book of the author's disciples:

> Christ is He who said to the Father, "Abba" (Mark 14:36). So how is it that our relationship with Him be on the level of metaphor or symbol, then we cry out [saying] the same words? How do we utter what we do not have and what we were not given? But because the true Son, our Lord Jesus, is the Son of the Father, "He took what is ours, and gave us what is His"—this being the praise and Doxology of the Church—, so He gave us the fellowship in His sonship.

We say that there is a substantial[701] difference between the sonship of Christ to the Father, and our sonship to the Father. Therefore, He is called the only begotten Son[702], because He is the only begotten of the essence of the Father and of His nature. As for us, we are sons by adoption, by grace. And great is the difference between adoption and sonship. We are sons by faith, as the Scripture says, "But as many as received Him, to them He gave the right to become children of God, to those who believe in His name."[703] We are also sons through love, as the Apostle says, "Behold what manner of love the Father has bestowed on us, that we should be called children of God!"[704]

We "received the Spirit of adoption by whom we cry out, 'Abba, Father,'"[705] not because we are like Him—and it is impossible to

---

701 I.e. of the essence.
702 See John 1:18; John 3:16, 18; 1 John 4:9.
703 John 1:12.
704 1 John 3:1.
705 Romans 8:15.

be like Him. He gave us a sonship to the Father which is other than His own sonship. Therefore, He is the Son of God by nature, and we are sons by adoption. And it is impossible for adoption to uplift us to deification. And we will not be equal to the Son in His sonship. The maximum to which we may reach is "to be conformed to the image of His Son."[706] We are created, but the Son is eternal[707]. And the creature is not deified, and the sonship which is given to us is not by our nature[708].

It is also said in Dr. Bibawy's book *Athanasius the Apostolic...*, "Partaking of the Divine nature is the obtaining of the gift of adoption through the Son. And the rejection of this is an explicit return to Judaism."

We do not reject the adoption but believe in it. We, however, reject the adoption as a sign for the partaking in the Divine nature, where we receive deification by the adoption.

Judaism, also, did not at all reject the adoption. It was said concerning Adam that he is "the son of God,"[709] and it was said of the seed of Seth and Enosh that they were children of God. It was said concerning this seed, in the beginning of the story of the Flood, "the sons of God saw the daughters of men, that they were beautiful."[710] And God did not forbid the title of sonship from those who rebelled against Him, for He said at the beginning of the prophecy of Isaiah, "I have nourished and brought up children, and they have rebelled against Me."[711] And Isaiah testifies, saying, "But now, O LORD, You are our Father."[712] Sonship to God is present then since the Old Testament, so we should not say that rejecting the adoption is a return to Judaism. For Paul the Apostle says concerning the Jews, "who are Israelites, to whom pertain the

---

706   Romans 8:29.
707   Arabic: *azali*, that is, from everlasting, without beginning.
708   "Not by our nature" is literally "from outside our nature."
709   Luke 3:38.
710   Genesis 6:2.
711   Isaiah 1:2.
712   Isaiah 64:8.

adoption, the glory, the covenants, the giving of the law."[713]

There is no relationship at all, however, between adoption and deification. For we say to God "Our Father," and at the same time we say to Him, "We are Your servants and Your creation." And we are not deified! The Lord says at the last day to every faithful, wise steward of His stewards, "Well done, good and faithful servant; you were faithful over a few things, I will make you ruler over many things. Enter into the joy of your lord."[714] No matter how good and faithful he is, he is still a servant, and his reward is to enter into the joy of his lord, without being deified.

Therefore, humble yourselves, O sons. And for the sake of the salvation of your souls, I say to you, do not [seek to] be deified. Do not think of yourselves more highly than you ought[715].

5. Is the resurrection from the dead the partaking in the Divine nature?

The resurrection of the Lord Christ signifies His Divinity, for He is the only One who arose by His will and His power, and no one raised Him up. As for the people who arose from the dead, they arose by a power outside themselves. And so will the resurrection at the last day be too. It will be through a miracle by God Himself and will not signify at all the deification of those whom the Lord will raise.

Dr. Bibawy, however, sees that the resurrection is a partaking in the Divinity! So he says in his book about St. Athanasius, "The meaning of partaking in the Divine nature … a partaking in eternal life and incorruptibility … and this is the partaking in the Divine nature, because it is a partaking in Christ who is risen from the dead," [and continues] till he says, "a partaking in the Divinity, because eternal life is the life of God Himself."

And nearly the same expressions appear in the book of the

---

713 Romans 9:4.
714 Matthew 25:21.
715 See Romans 12:3.

author's disciples, where it is said, "Eternal life is the life of God Himself, and our partaking in this life is a partaking in God Himself, according to the words of John the Apostle," and is also said, "Eternal life is the life of God Himself. And if this were not a partaking in the nature of God, that is, the life of God, then what would it be?" That is, the partaking in eternal life is the partaking in the nature of God, which is a kind of deification. The following also appeared in the same book, "that He may grant man steadfastness in not dying and immortality, through the partaking in the Divinity."

We answer these, [by saying], that the life of God is from His same nature. But for us, it is a gift from God through His grace. So we must not take the gift as a proof for deification. Therefore, we say in the Divine Liturgy, "upon those … bestowing eternal life." Also the people who are enjoying eternal life were dead before the resurrection. And this death is in conflict with deification. The righteous who rise from the dead will live with God in the heavenly Jerusalem, about which it is said, "The tabernacle of God is with men,"[716] and not, "the tabernacle of God is with gods." For after the resurrection, they will remain men as they were on earth.

And they say that the resurrection of Christ is the deification of the humanity. This statement is theologically unacceptable. For the humanity will remain humanity after the resurrection. And the Lord Christ, after His resurrection, kept the title "the Son of Man." Also the deification of the humanity means the dissolution of the humanity. And this is against the Faith.

6. Is the partaking[717] in the Divinity revealed in the power over the demons?

This is clear in Dr. Bibawy's book, for he says, "Partaking in the Divine nature is clearly revealed in man's power over the demons, and in heaven in the life of incorruptibility." And we say that

---

716 Revelation 21:3.
717 Or: fellowship.

prevailing against the devil is a gift from God[718], and not [because of] man's deification. It is clear in the Book of Revelation[719], that the Archangel Michael prevailed against the devil and cast him to the earth. So, is this a proof of the deification of the Archangel Michael too? And numerous are the saints who prevailed against the demons, and those who had the gift of casting out demons, so is this considered deification of all these? Prevailing against the devil comes by humility, and not by deification.

7. Do we partake in the Divine nature in the Eucharist?

Dr. Bibawy says in his book on St. Athanasius, "Partaking of the Eucharist as a partaking[720] in the Divine nature," and he says, "The truth of our partaking in the Divinity because of our obtaining this heavenly Mystery which grants eternal life." And he also says, "Here the fellowship in the Divine nature reaches its goal, and it is man's obtaining … the heavenly, immortal, divine Mysteries."

And in their book, they say, "Marvelous! Behold, we drink the Divinity—of course, mystically—and we drink the life-giving Blood, according to grace." This is truly marvelous, for the Divinity is not eaten nor drunk. But the Divine Mysteries in the Mystery of the Eucharist are not given to us to partake in the Divinity— God forbid! Rather It is given "for salvation, remission of sins, and eternal life to those who partake of Him,"[721] and, "unto the purification of our souls, bodies, and spirits,"[722] as we say in the Divine Liturgy.

If the communicant drinks the Divinity, what about those who partake [of Communion] in an unworthy manner?[723] If the communicant were to eat and drink the Divinity, undoubtedly he would come out of Communion having become a God. And

---

718 See Matthew 10:1.
719 See Revelation 12:7–9.
720 Or: fellowship.
721 The Divine Liturgy According to St. Basil – The Confession.
722 The Divine Liturgy According to St. Basil – Prayer Before the Seven Short Litanies.
723 See 1 Corinthians 11.

the Holy Mysteries would not be worshipped, but people would worship the communicant! And if they protest with the unity between the Divinity and the humanity, this does not mean that man eats the Divinity. The example of blood is before us. The Scripture says, "The life of the flesh is in the blood,"[724] so the one who eats or drinks the blood is not eating the life [or soul] with it.

8. Did God become Man, that man may become a God?

If this phrase were taken as it appears, the purpose of the Incarnation would have been the deification of man. But it is known that God became Man for the redemption of man, and not his deification. And this is very evident in St. Athanasius' book *On the Incarnation of the Word*, and also evident from the saying of the Apostle concerning the Father, that He "sent His Son to be the propitiation for our sins."[725] Therefore, I see that we ought to say that God became the Son of Man, that man may become a son of God, with the redemption remaining the principal reason for the Incarnation.

---

724 Leviticus 17:11 and see Leviticus 17:14.
725 1 John 4:10.

CHAPTER FOURTEEN

On the Union of the Divinity with the Humanity

Introduction

Since some of those calling for the deification of man do not fully comprehend the nature of the union between the Divinity and the humanity in the Incarnation of the Lord Christ—glory be to Him—I perceived that it was necessary to write this article, to explain this truth to them, and so that they are not wise in their own eyes.

We all believe in the union of the Divinity with the humanity, in a union in which the Divinity parted not from the humanity for a single moment, nor a twinkling of an eye. And we believe that this union was accomplished without mingling, without confusion, and without alteration. So what does the phrase "without alteration" mean? It means that the Divinity was not altered to become a humanity, but kept all its characteristics and attributes. And likewise the humanity too was not altered to become a Divinity.

We will provide many examples to make this point clear. Despite the union of the Divinity with the humanity in the Incarnation of the Lord Christ, we note the following.

1. It was said concerning His humanity that He grew.

So it was said concerning the Lord Christ in His childhood, "And Jesus increased in wisdom and stature, and in favor with God and men,"[726] and it was also said, "And the Child grew and became strong in spirit, filled with wisdom."[727]

He, in His humanity, grew. As for the Divinity, it is impossible for it to grow, because it is at the pinnacle of perfection always, or in the absolute perfection. The Divinity is united with the humanity, not separating from it for a single moment. Nevertheless, the humanity grows, and the Divinity does not grow. For it is of the attributes of the Divinity that It does not grow. No one, then, should foolishly consider that the difference between the Divinity and the humanity on the subject of growth is a separation between the Divinity and the humanity.

2. It was said concerning the Lord Christ that He came into the world in the flesh and left it in the flesh.

He said to His disciples, "I came forth from the Father and have come into the world. Again, I leave the world and go to the Father."[728]

The phrase "[I] have come into the world" applies, of course, to the humanity only. As for the Divinity, it is said concerning It, "He was in the world, and the world was made through Him."[729] And in the same theological understanding, we treat the phrase "I leave the world." For the Lord Christ said it with respect to the flesh. With respect to the Divinity, He said, "Lo, I am with you always, even to the end of the age,"[730] and He also said, "Where two or three are gathered together in My name, I am there in the midst of them."[731]

Therefore, there is no contradiction between the phrases "I

---

726 Luke 2:52.
727 Luke 2:40.
728 John 16:28.
729 John 1:10.
730 Matthew 28:20.
731 Matthew 18:20.

leave the world" and "I am with you" in your midst. Rather, one was said concerning the humanity and the other concerning the Divinity, without any separation between the Divinity and the humanity.

Therefore, beware, O sons, for the Lord Christ says, "You are mistaken, not knowing the Scriptures."[732]

3. It was said concerning the Lord Christ that He ascended into heaven in the flesh.

And so it is said in the Divine Liturgy according to St. Gregory, "And at Your Ascension into the heavens in the body."[733] And so also it was said concerning Him in the book of Acts[734], "He was taken up, and a cloud received Him out of their sight," "who was taken up from you into heaven," and, "they looked steadfastly toward heaven as He went up."

As for the Divinity, It is not taken up into heaven nor does It ascend. It is present in heaven, on earth, and in that which is in between. It does not move from one place to another, because It is present everywhere, at the same time.

If it were said that the humanity ascended bodily and that the Divinity does not ascend, this does not mean at all [that there is] a separation of the Divinity from the humanity. Without a doubt, when the Lord Christ ascended into heaven in the flesh, His Divinity was united with His humanity without separation. But the ascension was attributed to the humanity only, because ascension is not of the attributes of the Divinity which is present everywhere.

"He who has ears to hear, let him hear!"[735]

---

732 Matthew 22:29.
733 The Divine Liturgy According to St. Gregory – Prayer of Reconciliation.
734 Acts 1:9–11.
735 Matthew 13:43.

4. It was said concerning the Lord Christ, in more than one place, that He slept.

This took place when He was in the boat, and a great disturbance arose on the sea, so that the waves were covering the boat, "but He was in the stern, asleep on a pillow. And they awoke Him and said to Him, 'Teacher, do You not care that we are perishing?'"[736] The story of His sleeping in the boat also appears in the Gospel according to St. Luke.[737]

And without a doubt, this sleep was said concerning the humanity only, because the Divinity "shall neither slumber nor sleep."[738] And although sleep belongs to the humanity only, and not the Divinity, yet His Divinity was fully united with His humanity, as evidenced by that He arose and rebuked the wind, and with authority "said to the sea, 'Peace, be still!' And the wind ceased and there was a great calm.... and [they] said to one another, 'Who can this be, that even the wind and the sea obey Him!'"[739]

Here the Divinity is united with the humanity without separation. Sleep and waking up, however, were attributed to the humanity only, because sleep is not of the attributes of the Divinity.

"He who has ears to hear, let him hear!"[740]

5. It was said concerning the humanity of the Lord Christ that He hungered and thirsted.

It was said, in His fasting forty days on the mount of temptation, that "in those days He ate nothing, and afterward, when they had ended, He was hungry."[741] This was also mentioned in the Gospel according to St. Matthew: "And when He had fasted forty days and forty nights, afterward He was hungry."[742]

---

736 Mark 4:38.
737 Luke 8:23–24.
738 Psalms 121:4.
739 Mark 4:39–41.
740 Matthew 13:43.
741 Luke 4:2.
742 Matthew 4:2.

He was hungry in His humanity and was tempted in His humanity, although His Divinity was united with it, as evidenced by that when He rebuked the devil and said to him, "'Away with you, Satan!' ... Then the devil left Him, and behold, angels came and ministered to Him."[743] Nevertheless, hunger is attributed to the humanity, because hunger is not of the attributes of the Divinity. The Divinity did not share in the hunger; nevertheless, this does not at all mean that the Divinity was separated from the humanity.

The same words are said concerning the thirst of the Lord Christ. For He said on the cross, "I thirst!"[744] The Divinity neither hungers nor thirsts, and consequently, the Divinity does not eat nor drink. And this does not at all prevent that the Divinity be united with the humanity, not separating from it for a single moment, nor a twinkling of an eye. But Its attributes and characteristics were not lost in uniting with the humanity.

6. It was also said concerning the Lord Christ that He was wearied.

In the account of His meeting the Samaritan woman, it was said of Him, "Jesus therefore, being wearied from His journey, sat thus by the well."[745] The Divinity does not become wearied. And without a doubt, the Lord was wearied in the flesh, though it was united with the Divinity.

The Divinity, in its union with the humanity, did not deprive Him of the attributes of the flesh, nor its weaknesses, that of being wearied and in pain, of hunger and thirst, of the need for rest and sleep. And the Divinity did not deprive Him of the need for eating and drinking. That is because He resembled our nature in everything, except for sin alone.

7. It was also said concerning the Lord Christ that He suffered. And this is a doctrine.

---

743 Matthew 4:10–11.
744 John 19:28.
745 John 4:6.

He Himself said to His disciples before the cross, "that He must go to Jerusalem, and suffer many things from the elders and chief priests and scribes, and be killed, and be raised the third day."[746] And after the resurrection, He said to His disciples, "Thus it is written, and thus it was necessary for the Christ to suffer and to rise from the dead the third day."[747] It was said of Him in the epistle to the Hebrews that "suffered outside the gate,"[748] and that, "For in that He Himself has suffered, being tempted, He is able to aid those who are tempted."[749] Verses concerning His suffering are very many, which include the striking with the palms of the hands, scourging, crucifixion, nails, thorns, and many other matters as in Psalm 22[750].

Nevertheless, the Divinity does not suffer. Whoever says that the Divinity suffers falls into a heresy. In all the suffering of Christ, His Divinity was united with His humanity, and did not separate from it for a single moment, nor a twinkling of an eye.

8. Christ also died—died in His humanity. But the Divinity does not die.

Nevertheless, in its [i.e. the humanity's] death, it was united with the Divinity and did not part from It. And we say to Him in the litanies of the Ninth Hour [of the Agpeya], "O You, who tasted death in the flesh in the ninth hour…" and we say in the Syrian Fraction [in the Divine Liturgy] concerning the death of Christ, "His soul parted from His body, even though His Divinity never parted, either from His soul or from His body."

Death is of the attributes of the humanity and is not of the attributes of the Divinity. And [the fact that] death is not of the attributes of the Divinity, does not at all mean that the Divinity parted from the humanity. Despite the union of the Divinity with

---

746 Matthew 16:21.
747 Luke 24:46.
748 Hebrews 13:12.
749 Hebrews 2:18.
750 See Psalms 22:7–18.

the humanity, the Divinity kept its attributes, in that the Divinity does not become weary, suffer pain, die, grow, ascend, thirst, hunger, nor sleep, as we have previously explained.

9. With the same rationale, we say that the Divinity is neither eaten nor drunk, in the Mystery of the Eucharist, despite the union of the Divinity with the humanity.

When the Lord presented this Mystery to the disciples, He said to them, "Take, eat; this is My body.... Drink from it, all of you. For this is My blood."[751] And He did not mention the phrase "My Divinity" at all.

Likewise, St. Paul the Apostle said, "The cup of blessing which we bless, is it not the communion of the blood of Christ? The bread which we break, is it not the communion of the body of Christ?"[752] And in this manner, he taught concerning the communion of the body and blood, and not communion *in the Divinity*, as those say who call for the deification of man. Truly the Divinity of Christ parted not from His humanity, yet also the Divinity is not eaten nor drunk, for this is one of Its attributes.

St. Paul the Apostle repeated the same word of the Lord in handing down this Mystery to the disciples. Then he said, "Therefore whoever eats this bread or drinks this cup of the Lord in an unworthy manner will be guilty of the body and blood of the Lord.... For he who eats and drinks in an unworthy manner eats and drinks judgment to himself, not discerning the Lord's body."[753] He did not at all refer to His Divinity while talking about the danger of partaking of Communion in an unworthy manner, but said, "[He] will be guilty of the body and blood of the Lord," and was satisfied [and said no more].

The Lord Christ says concerning this Mystery, "For My flesh is food indeed, and My blood is drink indeed. He who eats My

---

751 Matthew 26:26–28. See also Mark 14:22–24.
752 1 Corinthians 10:16.
753 1 Corinthians 11:27, 29.

flesh and drinks My blood abides in Me, and I in him."[754] And He did not say, "He who eats and drinks My Divinity." This is because the Divinity is not eaten nor drunk despite its union with the humanity. Therefore, do not proclaim strange teachings, which have not appeared in the Holy Scriptures nor in the writings of the Fathers. The Fathers also gave us an example for the union of the humanity with the Divinity, as the union of heated iron with fire[755], and as the union of the spirit with the body[756]. "He who has ears to hear, let him hear!"[757]

As for the Lord's saying "abides in Me, and I in him," this does not mean abiding in His Divinity. For those who partook of Communion for the first time at the Lord's supper did not abide [in Him]. For some of them were afraid and ran away; one of them denied Him three times, and they all hid in the upper room out of fear of the Jews. The phrase "abides in Me, and I in him," the Lord also explained in the Gospel according to St. John when He said to His Apostles, "Abide in My love. If you keep My commandments, you will abide in My love."[758] And He did not talk about abiding in His Divinity.

My advice to you, my sons: humble yourselves and do not [seek to] be deified. And do not think in yourselves that you have become the guardians of Orthodoxy or the guardians of the sayings of the Fathers. Always remember the saying of the Scripture, "Pride goes before destruction, and a haughty spirit before a fall."[759] For until now, I still hold fast to the saying of the Didascalia, "Obliterate sin by teaching."[760] And I still have compassion on you, so I wish that you would have compassion on yourselves, of what you are in.

---

754 John 6:55–56.
755 See Cyril of Alexandria, *A Commentary upon the Gospel According to S. Luke* 2, R.P. Smith, trans. (Oxford, ENG: At the University Press, 1859), 667.
756 See Cyril of Alexandria, *Letters 1-50*, J.I. McEnerney, trans. (Washington, D.C.: The Catholic University of America Press, 1987), 214. Also ibid., 193.
757 Matthew 13:43.
758 John 15:9–10.
759 Proverbs 16:18.
760 Cf. *The Didascalia Apostolorum in English*, M.D. Gibson, trans. (London, UK: Cambridge University Press, 1903), 33.

CHAPTER FIFTEEN

Against Biblical Criticism

The danger of biblical criticism

Some of the teachers of the Scriptures and preachers in the West make themselves judges[761] of the Holy Scriptures: they review its words as though they were scholars of language, they criticize whatever they wish, and they delete whatever they wish to also. It is as though the Scriptures were subject to their minds, and not their minds are the ones that ought to be subject to the Scriptures. They also made some parts [of the Scriptures] less important than others.

We neither accept this from them, nor do we agree with them concerning it. That some of their ideas would be transmitted into our Church is a matter that makes one wonder, and we never expected it at all. We are obliged to face them, so that they do not reach some of the simple people who may accept the ideas presented to them without examination.

1. Entry into Jerusalem

As the author raised a problem on the subject of redemption around the phrase "crucified for us[762] and died for us," and said that this is a theologically wrong translation—and we have responded to this in "How was the Redemption of Humankind Accomplished?"—

---

761 Or: those who evaluate and rectify.
762 Or: on our behalf.

likewise he raised a problem on the entry of the Lord into Jerusalem on Hosanna Sunday. And this is around the following.

A donkey and a colt—or a colt only?

The Gospel according to St. Matthew says:

> Now when they drew near Jerusalem, and came to Bethphage, at the Mount of Olives, then Jesus sent two disciples, saying to them, "Go into the village opposite you, and immediately you will find a donkey tied, and a colt with her. Loose them and bring them to Me. And if anyone says anything to you, you shall say, 'The Lord has need of them,' and immediately he will send them." All this was done that it might be fulfilled which was spoken by the prophet, saying: "Tell the daughter of Zion, 'Behold, your King is coming to you, lowly, and sitting on a donkey, a colt, the foal of a donkey.'" So the disciples went and did as Jesus commanded them. They brought the donkey and the colt, laid their clothes on them, and set Him on them.[763]

It is clear from the account of St. Matthew the Evangelist that the phrase "a donkey and a colt" is repeated three times, and that the use of plural is repeated six times. The author, however, denies that and says in his biblical criticism that Christ did not use except a colt only. So how did that happen?

Did Matthew the Evangelist make a mistake on the entry of Christ into Jerusalem?

The author confesses that there is a mistake—but [even] mistakes. He says that St. Matthew took [what he wrote] from the prophecy of Zechariah, and that there is a mistake in understanding Zechariah. Also the scribes made a mistake, and after them the translators; and Matthew was obliged to modify meanings and words, to be in

---

[763] Matthew 21:1–7.

plural. Then he compared it with the Gospel according to St. John (12:15). Thus he says in his interpretation of the Gospel according to St. John:

> St. John took the word from its origin which is written in the book of Zechariah: "Rejoice greatly, O daughter of Zion! Shout, O daughter of Jerusalem! Behold, your King is coming to you; He is just and having salvation, lowly and riding on a donkey, and on a colt, the foal of a donkey" (Zechariah 9:9).

The author continues, saying:

> It is known in the prophetic, Jewish literature, especially that which came in poems, that the repetition of speech comes to enhance the tune and rhythm, and to clarify the meaning. The repetition in this verse is made clear here: First "O daughter of Zion" and "O daughter of Jerusalem;" then he repeated "riding on a donkey." Then he desired to clarify that it was a young donkey, "the foal of a donkey." The scribes then made a mistake, and after them, the translators. And they wrote, "on a donkey, and on a colt, the foal of a donkey." And they added an "and," so the speech came wrong. And it is as though He were sitting on a donkey and a colt, together. And what is correct is that He [sat] on a young donkey, that is, a colt.

After that the author attributes the mistake to St. Matthew in writing his Gospel, but [to the extent] that he modified the meanings and words on purpose. So he says:

> But as the scribes understood the Septuagint, so did St. Matthew copy from it into his Gospel, the way it was. And he was obliged to modify meanings and words, to be in plural. That is, a donkey and a colt, together. So it came thus: "'...and immediately you will find a donkey tied, and a colt with her. Loose them and bring them to Me. And if anyone says anything to you, you shall say, "The Lord has need of them," and immediately he will send them.'

All this was done that it might be fulfilled which was spoken by the prophet, saying: 'Tell the daughter of Zion, "Behold, your King is coming to you, lowly, and sitting on a donkey, a colt, the foal of a donkey"'" (Matthew 21:2–5).

So did the great St. Matthew fabricate the words and modify the prophecy? Or did the method of biblical criticism lead to all this?

Did Mark and Luke then make a mistake too?

The author says, "This unintentional mistake by copying, each of the saints Mark, Luke, John avoided, where they mentioned that it was one colt only. And each of the saints Mark and Luke adds the phrase 'on which no one has sat' (Mark 11:2; Luke 19:30)."

Nevertheless, neither St. Mark nor St. Luke escaped biblical criticism, for the author says in his interpretation of the Gospel according to St. Matthew, "St. Mark is distinguished by saying that the colt on which no one has sat. And this is impossible, for training the colt is inevitable, through one riding it in the past. Otherwise riding it would be impossible. So what is the matter?"

Was this young animal going to rebel against the Lord Christ if He were to ride it without their having trained it, so that the author said, "This is impossible"? Or is it an accusation against the description mentioned by St. Mark and St. Luke?

St. Matthew the Evangelist was an eyewitness

The author, however, in his biblical criticism, forgot an important truth, which is that St. Matthew the Evangelist was an eyewitness. He did not take [the information] from the prophecy of Zechariah, nor from the prophecy of Zephaniah. Likewise, he did not take from the Septuagint translation. But he himself saw everything concerning the entry of Christ into Jerusalem, and heard that which the disciples said. And he knew why Christ used a donkey and a colt, not so that He may ride them together [at the same time]. For this thing [using a donkey and a colt] is not of the imagination! He did this, rather, so that He may give rest to each of them in alternation, that one of them may not bear the whole distance alone: hills and valleys. When He entered Jerusalem, at that time He was riding the colt, as St. Mark described it.

The place of inspiration in writing the Gospels

Likewise, the one who goes into biblical criticism and attributes a mistake to one of the Evangelists, forgets something extremely important; that is, the place of inspiration in writing the Gospels. If they wrote the Gospels, "as they were moved by the Holy Spirit,"[764] as the Scripture says, from where would the mistake come? Is this an accusation against the divine inspiration? Or is it an accusation of the absence of inspiration? Or is it a warning to stay away from this kind of biblical criticism? "He who has ears to hear, let him hear!"[765]

2. Deletion of the end of the Gospel according to Mark

In the author's interpretation of the Gospel according to St. Mark, he stopped at Mark (16:8), deleting the last twelve verses of the Gospel, with the excuse that his conscience is at rest to stop at this point!

The author says in his interpretation of the Gospel of Mark:

> As for the remaining twelve verses ([after] 16:1–8), studies by meticulous scholars have proven that they had been lost from the Gospel and were rewritten by one of the seventy disciples, named Ariston. This disciple lived in the first century. And these twelve verses were collected by Ariston from the Gospel of St. John and the Gospel of St. Luke, with which to complete the resurrection.

And here we wonder: What is troubling his conscience in these

---

764 2 Peter 1:21.
765 Matthew 13:43.

twelve verses?

The appearance of the Lord to Mary Magdalene (Mark 16:9–11) is mentioned in the same chapter (Mark 16:1), and in Matthew (28:1) and John 20. So what is troubling him in that St. Mark mentions it again when he wanted to summarize the appearance occurrences?

The appearance of the Lord to two of the disciples (Mark 16:12–13) was mentioned in Luke 24 in much detail, and these are the disciples of Emmaus.

The Apostles' unbelief (Mark 16:14) was also mentioned in Luke 24. So what is in all these that troubles the conscience?

Is his conscience troubled by the saying of the Lord Christ to the Apostles, "Go into all the world and preach the gospel to every creature,"[766] or His saying to them, "He who believes and is baptized will be saved"[767]? All these are mentioned in Matthew: "Go therefore and make disciples of all the nations, baptizing them in the name of the Father and of the Son and of the Holy Spirit."[768]

Or is his conscience troubled by the signs which the Lord promised His disciples to perform? And such signs are abundant, as they were mentioned in the book of Acts of the Apostles and in others.

Or is his conscience troubled by, "So then, after the Lord had spoken to them, He was received up into heaven, and sat down at the right hand of God"[769]? His being received up into heaven was mentioned in Acts (1:9), which is a feast of the Lord we celebrate—the Feast of the Ascension. And His sitting down at the right hand of God is mentioned in Acts (7:55) and in many places in the epistle to the Hebrews and in the book of Psalms[770]. The Lord pointed to this psalm in Matthew (22:44). What is troubling his conscience in all these?

---

766 Mark 16:15.
767 Mark 16:16.
768 Matthew 28:19.
769 Mark 16:19.
770 See Psalms 110:1.

Or was it the last verse in the Gospel of Mark that troubled the conscience of the author, which said, "And they went out and preached everywhere, the Lord working with them and confirming the word through the accompanying signs,"[771]? This verse, however, is a summary of the whole book of Acts.

What troubles the conscience, however, is the sowing of doubt in the Gospel by deleting part of it, and the sowing of doubt in all that resembles this deleted part.

Not even the Protestants have dared do such a thing, who deleted Books from the Old Testament, nor have their interpreters of the Scriptures dared do so. Nor have Jehovah's Witnesses dared do so, who made a new translation of the Holy Scriptures that fits their beliefs.

Is this kind of biblical criticism going farther than many in its criticism? And does this criticism break that [commandment] for which a punishment was pronounced at the end of the Book of Revelation, concerning the one who deletes...! "He who has ears to hear, let him hear."[772]

3. "My God, My God, why have You forsaken Me?"

The author dealt with this verse in both of his interpretations of the Gospel of Matthew and the Gospel of Mark. The scriptural text is as follows: "And about the ninth hour Jesus cried out with a loud voice, saying, 'Eli, Eli, lama sabachthani?' that is, 'My God, My God, why have You forsaken Me?'"[773]

The author said in his interpretation of the Gospel of Matthew:

Then it is necessary that the Son suffers the death of the body, considering that He is one with His body. Here the difficulty and the impossibility come from the substantial[774] connection with the life of the Father. Therefore, any death

---

771 Mark 16:20.
772 Matthew 13:43.
773 Matthew 27:46.
774 I.e. of the essence.

the Son suffers, even in the body, reaches the connection between the Father and the Son. Thus, here, for the Son to die in the body, it is inevitable that the Father forsakes the incarnate Son, that He may die. Otherwise, the death of the Son in the body would be impossible.

He also says, "And this is a part of the dreadful things the Son suffered in Gethsemane, that He may become a sin? For it is inevitable that He becomes estranged from the Father," and, "Now the hour of death has come, and the Father forsook the Son, that He may go through death in the body while He is the Lord of life."

We say [in response] that the Father did not forsake the Son [not even] for a single moment. For there is no separation between the hypostases of the Holy Trinity. Also, the union between the Father and the Son does not prevent the death of the Son in the flesh. The Son said, "I am in the Father and the Father in Me."[775] Therefore, it is impossible that there be forsaking or separation. St. Paul the Apostle says that Christ is "the power of God and the wisdom of God,"[776] so were the wisdom of God and His power separated from Him on the cross? Absolutely not! Nor were they separated when the Son said to the Father "why have You forsaken Me," as we will explain later.

We say also that the Divinity of the Son is equal to the Divinity of the Father. They are one Divinity, as He said before, "I and My Father are one."[777] So what is the meaning of "it is inevitable that the Father forsakes the incarnate Son, that He may die. Otherwise, the death of the Son in the body would be impossible"? Therefore, did the Divinity of the Son forsake the incarnate Son? Impossible, because His Divinity parted not from his humanity for a single moment, nor a twinkling of an eye, according to the teaching of the Church. So, if His Divinity was united with it, what is the difference then between the Divinity of the Son and the Divinity of the Father?

---

775 John 14:10 and 14:11.
776 1 Corinthians 1:24.
777 John 10:30.

The Divinity of the Son did not forsake Him, and yet He died in the body. As we say in the Syrian Fraction, "His soul parted from His body, even though His Divinity never parted, either from His soul or from His body," even when He was in the tomb.

The phrase "The death of the Son in the body would be impossible unless the Father forsook Him" is wrong theologically without a doubt.

The author presents another interpretation for the phrase "My God, My God, why have You forsaken Me?" in his interpretation of the Gospel of Mark, saying:

> Then after that He is stripped, and crucified on the wood as a criminal, and spoken evil of among men. Here the shame reaches its great antithesis: How does the bearer of glory bear shame? And this is not a metaphorical nor ideological antithesis, but the antithesis of His essence, which is impossible to happen in any way whatsoever. For the shame of the Son surely befalls the Father! And shame is a curse; if it is inflicted on the Son, it is inflicted on the Father inevitably.

The author then continues in explaining his interpretation, and says:

> Therefore, if Christ had not revealed to us the mystery of the curse which He bore, the cross would have remained a theological riddle [which is] not accepted without offense. Here Christ unveiled how Christ endured the shame alone, when He raised His voice, crying out, that all may hear and that the Gospels, history, and the theologians may record, "My God, My God, why have You forsaken Me?" (Mark 15:34). This is the inevitable forsaking which God performed on the Christ, that it may be possible for Him to go through the curse alone for the sake of humanity which He bore.

We would like to say that the basis of this theory is wrong: for the curse of the Son does not befall the Father, neither does the shame of the Son befall the Father.

The curse of Cain did not befall Adam whom God blessed[778]. God said to Cain, "So now you are cursed from the earth, which has opened its mouth to receive your brother's blood from your hand.... A fugitive and a vagabond you shall be on the earth."[779] Nothing of all this, however, befell his father Adam.

Likewise, the curse of Canaan did not befall his father Noah, who said, "Cursed be Canaan; a servant of servants he shall be to his brethren."[780]

The shame of Esau, also, did not befall his father Isaac. St. Paul the Apostle said concerning Esau, "Lest there be any fornicator or profane person like Esau, who for one morsel of food sold his birthright."[781] This shame did not befall his father.

The shame of the sons of Jacob, also, who envied their brother and cast him into a well, sold him as a slave, and lied to their father and deceived him, saying, "A wild beast has devoured Joseph"[782]— all this shame did not befall their father Jacob at all.

The curse and shame, also, which befell the children of Israel did not befall Israel himself, nor their forefather Abraham.

Also the disobedient and rebellious son who is stubborn and disobeys his parents, the Law sentences him to death by stoning.[783] And his shame does not befall his parents.

And the shame of Absalom did not befall his father David. And examples such as these are numerous.

The saying of the author that the shame of the Son inevitably befalls the Father is erroneous and does not fit the teaching of the Scriptures; and applying this theory on the Father and the Son in

---

778 See Genesis 1:28.
779 Genesis 4:11.
780 Genesis 9:25.
781 Hebrews 12:16.
782 See Genesis 37.
783 See Deuteronomy 21:18–21.

the Holy Trinity is a graver error.

The death of Christ means the separation of the two elements of His humanity from each other, that is, the separation of His spirit from His body. And this does not mean the separation of His humanity from His Divinity, and does not mean at all the separation of the Divinity of the Father from the Divinity of the Son. Of the proofs that the Divinity did not separate from the humanity is that He "cried out with a loud voice, saying, 'Eli, Eli, lama sabachthani?' that is, 'My God, My God, why have You forsaken Me?'"[784] This loud voice the body was not capable of [making], the body which was extremely exhausted from the proceedings of the trial, the scourging, the crucifixion, the nails and thorns, and the continuation of all these and the labor until the ninth hour.

What is then the meaning of "My God, My God, why have You forsaken Me"?

The meaning is "Why have You left[785] Me to suffer?" And by "forsaking," it does not mean separation. And it is not according to the saying of the author, "This is the inevitable forsaking which God performed on the Christ, that it may be possible for Him to go through the curse alone."

The sound interpretation is that the Divinity, while united with the humanity, did not interfere to prevent pain from the humanity. Therefore, the humanity continued to endure the pain, then death, despite its union with the Divinity. As an example of this, approximately, is that it happened that a father takes his son to the doctor, to remove a thorn stuck in his hand or to clean an abscess he has. So, the son suffers and cries out to his father, saying, "Why have you forsaken me?" That is, "Why have you left me to suffer?" although the father was carrying him and holding him.

Another interpretation is that Christ desired to alert the Jews to Psalm 22, which starts by, "My God, My God, why have You

---

784 Matthew 27:46.
785 The Arabic word is exactly as it appears in the verse, that is, "forsaken."

forsaken Me?"[786] And this psalm includes prophecies concerning His crucifixion and suffering. It says in this psalm, "The congregation of the wicked has enclosed Me. They pierced My hands and My feet; I can count all My bones. They look and stare at Me. They divide My garments among them, and for My clothing they cast lots."[787] This psalm includes many other details that match the events of His crucifixion.

Another point concerning this whole subject is that the author confused between "the Son of Man" and "the Son of God." With respect to the Divinity, the Son of God did not die; rather we say concerning Him in the Agpeya, "tasted death in the flesh," that is died in the humanity. For God is living [and] does not die. And we say, "the living Christ." Likewise, the shame, curse, and the rest of these matters afflicted His humanity, and not His Divinity. It is like "iron heated with fire," which the Fathers mentioned. When you hammer the iron, which is heated with fire, the blows affect the iron and bend it, yet the fire [itself] is not affected by the blows.

---

[786] Psalms 22:1.
[787] Psalms 22:16–18.

CHAPTER SIXTEEN

The Interpretation of the Scriptures is as the Scriptures Themselves

The author says in his book, "The interpretation of the word is a state of inspiration which is no less than the utterance of it!" and, "The inference[788] of doctrine from the texts of the Scriptures is a work of divine inspiration which is no less than the laying down of the Scriptures themselves. For, in both instances, the mind reaches to facing the truth."

We marvel at this extreme boldness of speech! How is "the interpretation of the word is a state of inspiration which is no less than the utterance of it"? Concerning the utterance of the words of the Scriptures, St. Peter the Apostle said that they were not at all by the will of man, "but holy men of God spoke as they were moved by the Holy Spirit."[789] That is, they were inspired by God.[790] So, is everyone who interprets some verses from the Scriptures or extracts doctrine from them in a state of divine inspiration that is no less than [that of] the saintly Apostles' utterance of the verses of the Scriptures, and is in a state which is no less than [that of] the laying down of the Scriptures themselves?

Is it fitting that we spread this teaching amidst our children, or even amidst preachers so that they become conceited and say, "What is the difference between us and the evangelists Matthew,

---

788 Literally: extraction.
789 2 Peter 1:21.
790 Literally: That is, in a state of inspiration by God.

Mark, Luke, and John"?

And if some say that he meant the interpretation of the word on the level of the [Church] Fathers, we say that not even on the level of the Fathers either. Consider a great saint of the Fathers like St. John Chrysostom. Are his books of interpretation considered on the level of the Scriptures and no less than the utterance of them? And consider a great saint of the Fathers, heroes of the faith, like St. Athanasius the Apostolic. Is his inference of the doctrine from the texts of the Scriptures considered a divinely inspired work that is no less than the laying down of the Scriptures themselves?

These are hard sayings. Who can accept them from the theological aspect? Are all these sayings accepted by the committee for defending Orthodoxy? Are all the books of the Fathers which they quote on the level of the Scriptures? Or is this a disparagement of the value of the Scriptures?

CHAPTER SEVENTEEN

Other Church Mysteries, Besides the Seven Mysteries

The author writes in his book:

> There are in the Church many other mysteries, not counted as part of the seven Mysteries. These Mysteries, however, are not devoid of events of descent [of the Spirit] too. For example, during the consecration of monks, the Holy Spirit descends through prayer and works by His grace in the consecrated person, for the preservation of his chastity and death to the lusts of the world. And in the consecration of churches, the Holy Spirit descends through the prayer of the Bishop, to sanctify this place and devote it for prayer. And in the consecration of the water, the Holy Spirit descends to give power to the water for purification and healing, as in the Liturgy of the Blessing of the Water, and especially in Theophany, "the divine manifestation." And in the prayer of the dead, the Holy Spirit descends to receive His own temple.

Speaking of the Mysteries of the Church, other than the seven Mysteries, is contrary to that which we received from the Church, and that which we teach our children and youth. And this matter is no more than someone who is influenced by reading foreign books. We will give examples to respond to this opinion.

The consecration of churches is a branch of the Mystery of

Holy Myron. The use of the mystery of anointing came in the book of Exodus[791] to sanctify and consecrate the tabernacle of meeting and all its altars and holy utensils. Consecrating churches then is not a new mystery to be added to the Mystery of Anointing (the Mystery of Holy Myron), but it is a branch of it.

And the consecration of monks is not a new Mystery. Rather, it is the funeral prayer that is prayed on them, considering that the monk has died to the world.

And the prayer over the dead is not a mystery of the Church, in which "the Holy Spirit descends to receive His own temple[792], that is the body." For the Holy Spirit receives the soul, as we say, "This very soul, for whom, we are gathered…" As for the body, the grave receives it, and that which takes place after the burial.

And the consecration of the water is the blessing of the water.

---

791 See Exodus 30.
792 See 1 Corinthians 6:19.

CHAPTER EIGHTEEN

The Efficacy of the Mystery of Matrimony Spiritually

The author says in his book with respect to the work of the Holy Spirit in the Mystery of Matrimony:

> The husband assimilates all that is in his wife, not only the good that is in her or her good habits and inclination to good, but, through the help of the spirit of intimacy, he receives, in submission to the efficacy of the Mystery, all that is in his wife, even the mistakes, shortcomings, and every imperfection regardless of its kind. He receives all that he senses in her and makes it his own, so that it becomes part of his being.
>
> Likewise also, the wife receives, through the efficacy of the Mystery of Matrimony, all that is in her husband, of shortcomings and virtues, so that there is no longer anything that belongs to her husband that may be foreign to her body and mind. And when the Scripture says that the husband is the head of the wife, it indicates that the husband occupies the thinking of the wife: "Your desire shall be for your husband" (Genesis 3:16).

Is the efficacy of the work of the Holy Spirit in the Mystery of Matrimony that "the husband assimilates all that is in his wife.... even the mistakes, shortcomings, and every imperfection regardless of its kind," and he "makes it his own, so that it becomes part of his being"? Does the Holy Spirit help him make the mistakes and shortcomings as though they are part of his being? And does the wife, through the efficacy of the Mystery, receive "all that is in her husband, of shortcomings"?

"Father, forgive them, for they do not know what they do."[793]

---

793 Luke 23:34.

CHAPTER NINETEEN

Against the Doctrine of Redemption, A Soul in Place of a Soul

In the author's book about St. Paul the Apostle, when discussing "atonement through substitution," that is "punishment instead of punishment," the author spoke about that which was mentioned in the Book of Leviticus concerning unintentional sins, after which he said:

> Let the reader pay attention here. For the sin offering in the Old Testament was offered on behalf of the sinner, was slaughtered on behalf of the sinner, and died on behalf of the sinner. That is, the animal died on behalf of the sinner, that the sinner may not die. For here the animal died alone, and man did not die… and now, can this rite be transferred, with its form and meaning, to the truth of the redemption which Christ accomplished on the cross?

The author denies this understanding of redemption and says in the footnote:

> The Protestant church forcefully holds onto the "atonement through substitution" theory, that is, "Christ died on our behalf,"[794] meaning as a substitute for us. And although we do not want to go to, nor are we comfortable with, arguments in theology, but we are strongly compelled to clarify our position concerning this subject, due to the

---
794 Or: Christ died for us.

spiritual importance it harbors, to which the reader will have the greatest rest.

This understanding, which he denies, and with which he characterizes the Protestant, is the belief of all of us in the redemption! And it is that which St. Athanasius the Apostolic proclaimed in *On the Incarnation of the Word*, that Christ was crucified and died on our behalf, so that He redeems us. That is, Christ died in order for us to live.

But the author in his attack of the principle of "punishment instead of punishment" says:

> Here is a critical obstacle that prevents the application: all the sin offerings which the Old Testament specified, as we have previously alerted to repeatedly, work only in case of unintentional sins … that is not deliberately. As for intentional sins, or those which are premeditated and by the will, there is no sacrifice at all for them in all of the Law of Moses. Or said in a clearer way, it is impossible to atone or substitute soul for soul in case of intentional sins, and that is according to the Law of Moses. Here it is difficult, whether from near or far, to apply [this] on the sacrifice of Christ, for the sacrifice of Christ is a sacrifice for intentional sin first and all kinds of sins which the Old Testament falls short of and refrains from offering a sacrifice at all for them. Therefore, here it is impossible that the sacrifice of Christ to be counted in place of the sinner, on behalf of the sinner, nor instead of the sinner, because the sin is an intentional sin, and the sinner must surely die, and it is impossible that a sacrifice of any kind is offered on his behalf!

We would like to say, if the sinner must surely die and the sacrifice of Christ is impossible to be counted in place of the sinner nor instead of him, then there is no redemption, because redemption means that a soul dies on behalf of another soul. And the redemption of Christ for us is that He died on our behalf and instead of us.

The author repeats his understanding in his interpretation of the epistle to the Romans, saying, "The sacrifices were for temporary, individual forgiveness, for every sin per se, but for unintentional sin only, because the sin that is intentional by the will has no remission, no forgiveness, and no sacrifice in any way whatever."

This means we have all perished, because most of our sins are intentional sins. According to the author's opinion, the sinner must surely die, and there is no remission or forgiveness.

Intentional Sin

We will respond to the author's understanding in the following points:

✤ Did the Holy Scriptures not mention sacrifices for intentional sin, as the author says? What did the Holy Scriptures say concerning this?

✤ Examples of intentional sins which Christ bore.

✤ The danger of the phrase "the death of the sinner himself."

✤ Verses on the redemption of Christ.

It appears that the author took into consideration what came in the Book of Leviticus, chapters four and five, *only*. Nevertheless, sadly, he spoke about "all the sin offerings which the Old Testament specified, as we have previously alerted to repeatedly, work only in case of unintentional sin."

Let us see then that which came in the Old Testament and the books of Moses.

In the Book of Leviticus, he speaks of "the great day of atonement," saying concerning the high priest and the sacrifices he offers, "[Aaron shall] make atonement for himself and for his house.... [then] he shall make atonement for the Holy Place, because of the uncleanness of the children of Israel, and because of their transgressions, for all their sins; and so he shall do for the tabernacle of meeting which remains among them in the midst of their uncleanness."[795] Therefore, are there no intentional sins among all the uncleanness of the children of Israel, all their transgressions, and all their sins, in the entire celebration of the great day of atonement?

Isaiah the prophet says concerning the sacrifice of Christ, "All we like sheep have gone astray; we have turned, everyone, to his own way; and the LORD has laid on Him the iniquity of us all."[796] Does "the iniquity of us all" not include intentional sins also?

St. Paul the Apostle repeats the same phrase concerning the Lord Christ, saying, "Who gave Himself for us, that He might redeem us from every lawless deed."[797] "Every lawless deed" includes both intentional and unintentional sins together.

St. John the Apostle says also, "The blood of Jesus Christ His Son cleanses us from all sin."[798]

The Lord Christ was incarnate, and emptied Himself, and took the form of a servant, and suffered and died on the cross—were all these for the sake of unintentional sins only? Are the unintentional sins only those for which sacrifices are offered [and] then the sacrifice of Christ? As for intentional sin, as the author says, no sacrifice is offered for them at all, but the sinner surely dies!

What about the sin of David the prophet[799], who committed adultery, devised schemes to conceal his sin, which failed, and then devised the killing of the woman's husband, and he himself married her—were all these not intentional sins? And David said, "Wash me, and I shall be whiter than snow."[800] And when he confessed his sin, Nathan the prophet said to him, "The LORD also has put away your sin; you shall not die."[801] Where did the Lord put away his sin? Is it not to the cross of Christ on Golgotha? Or did David die without a sacrifice for his sins? And what about the sins of the

---

795 Leviticus 16:11–16.
796 Isaiah 53:6.
797 Titus 2:14.
798 1 John 1:7.
799 See 2 Samuel 11.
800 Psalms 51:7.
801 2 Samuel 12:13.

fathers who reposed in hope, and whose sins were intentional?

The sacrifices that were offered for the people concerning their marrying foreigners in the days of Nehemiah and Ezra[802]—were they not for intentional sins, for they did not marry foreign women unintentionally?

What about that which came in the Book of Jeremiah the prophet, "I will forgive their iniquity, and their sin I will remember no more"[803]—was this for unintentional sins only?

What about that which came in the psalm, "Blessed is he whose transgression is forgiven, whose sin is covered. Blessed is the man to whom the LORD does not impute iniquity"[804]? This verse which Paul the Apostle quoted[805], and which we chant in [the service of] the consecration of new monks—are these concerning unintentional [sins] only, and not intentional [sins]. How does the Lord not impute iniquity to them? Is this not through sacrifice?

Most of the sins of men are intentional sins, for which the Lord Christ died, without saying to those who committed them, "You must surely die."

This is the teaching of the New Testament, for St. John the beloved says that God "loved us and sent His Son to be the propitiation for our sins."[806] And he says, "He Himself is the propitiation for our sins, and not for ours only but also for the whole world."[807] Do the sins of the whole world not include intentional sins, for which Christ died? So how does the author say, "It is impossible to atone or substitute soul for soul in case of intentional sin"? And how does the author say, "It is impossible that the sacrifice of Christ to be counted in place of the sinner, on behalf of the sinner, nor instead of the sinner"?

---

802 See Nehemiah 10:33.
803 Jeremiah 31:34.
804 Psalms 32:1–2.
805 See Romans 4:7–8.
806 1 John 4:10.
807 1 John 2:2.

Was worshipping the gold calf in the days of Moses[808] an intentional or unintentional sin? Likewise, worshipping the calf in the days of Rehoboam[809] and all the worshipping of idols? And all the sins of Communism and atheism, from which people repented, and what the Scripture calls, "the sins of the whole world"?

Were the sins of Augustine the philosopher unintentional or intentional sins? Likewise also the sins of Mary of Egypt?

What about the saying of the Scripture, "that God was in Christ reconciling the world to Himself, not imputing their trespasses to them"[810]?

And what about the saying of the Lord in the book of Ezekiel the prophet, "I will cleanse you from all your filthiness,"[811] and, "I will deliver you from all your uncleannesses"[812]? Would He deliver them without sacrifices?

As for the death of the sinner for himself, it is not considered a redemption, but a recompense. Does the right-hand thief say, "I have died for myself, and Christ did not die for me!"

Regarding the author's statement concerning our fellowship in the redemptive sufferings of Christ, in the same book about Paul the Apostle[813], it is contrary to the saying of the Scripture concerning the Lord Christ, "I have trodden the winepress alone, and from the peoples no one was with Me."[814]

If the sinner shall surely die, where is the redemption then? And if he died with Christ on the cross, why does he die once again in Baptism[815]? The adulterers did not ascend the cross to die with Christ on Golgotha. Christ did not take their bodies and die through them, as the author says. "He who has ears to hear, let him hear!"[816]

---

808 Exodus 32.
809 1 Kings 12.
810 2 Corinthians 5:19.
811 Ezekiel 36:25.
812 Ezekiel 36:29.
813 Arabic text adds: page 283.
814 Isaiah 63:3.
815 See Romans 6 and Colossians 2:12.
816 Matthew 13:43.

CHAPTER TWENTY

Concerning the Author's Book on the Sins of the Flesh

Introduction

This is a small book, or rather a booklet, of about eighteen pages. With this book, the author intended to console the sinners who have fallen into sins of the flesh. It was first published as an opening article in the Journal of Mark in November 1994, and then it was turned into a book. It included many details which are in disagreement with the biblical, spiritual approach.

We care about comforting the weary souls, but it is important that we give them comfort in a sound way. Therefore, we do not say to them, "Do not care nor be sorrowful because of the falls of the flesh, for all your sins were destroyed[817] when Christ bore them on the cross."

Comforting the weary souls because of their sins comes through guidance [leading] to repentance, through saying that the door of repentance is open to all. If the sinner is not able to do so, then he must pray and say to the Lord, "Restore me, and I will return,"[818] so grace would assist him to repent. And through repentance, his sins are forgiven him, and God erases them.

As for taking lightly the danger of the sins of the flesh, this is

---
817 Literally: died.
818 Jeremiah 31:18.

not a biblical teaching; nor is the saying that the commandments of God are for "the new man" only; nor is it when we comfort the sinner by [saying] that sorrow for sins is of the work of the devil who pollutes him "with the conscience of sin."

1. Are the commandments of the New Testament difficult to fulfill?

The author starts his letter to comfort the weary soul by saying, "The commandments of Christ are difficult, and who could fulfill them?" And he gave examples such as the love for enemies, and doing good to those who spitefully use you, going two miles with the one who compels you to go for one mile, and examples of such commandments. And [he said] that man cannot fulfill these commandments, and even the Apostles of the Lord themselves were not at the measure of fulfilling these commandments; and that if they were directed to the body, man is necessarily defeated. And he said:

> You read these commandments, so you find yourself a worm and not a man. And you throw yourself on the ground and confess your weakness, saying to the Lord, "I have measured myself against the measure of Your teaching and commandments, so I found myself to be a worm and not a man; I am dust and ashes. I do not have the ability to behold nor approach Your perfection, which is Yours in Your commandments. Does the dust make for himself a ladder, with which to ascend to Your heaven?" So, Christ and the Father would be fully satisfied by these words, by this conduct, and by this defeat.

We respond to this, by saying that God does not give us commandments which we cannot fulfill. Look! John the Apostle says, "His commandments are not burdensome."[819] Also we cannot separate the sublimity of the commandments from the work of grace in us and the work of the Holy Spirit with us. Alongside

---

819 1 John 5:3.

the commandments of the Lord, we remember the saying of St. Paul, "I can do all things through Christ who strengthens me."[820] Likewise if we read the history and the accounts of the fathers, we would find many, highly sublime examples of the fulfillment of these commandments.

Also, there is a difference between the commandments that belong to perfection and the negativity in the falls and sins of the body. So what does the author say concerning the sins of the body? He says, "These commandments were not given for the body."

2. Are these commandments not for the body, but for the new man?

He says, "Man has mistakenly understood that these commandments and teachings belong to the body, and that he should fulfill them on the level of this body and the old man[821], although they are sent only to the new man in Christ, who is renewed by the Holy Spirit." He also says, "But by the capabilities of the body, he is inevitably defeated. For Christ said, 'the flesh profits nothing' (John 6:63)." This phrase the Lord Christ said when speaking about Communion, and not with respect to the fulfillment of the commandments.

The author continues, saying, "It is evident that the commandments and teachings are sent to the new man. They are spiritual teachings for eternal life. And the new man is alive through the Holy Spirit."

We marvel at his separating the body from the spirit concerning the commandments. For God created man a spirit and body, united. And man will be judged before Him on the sins of the body and the spirit, together. Therefore, the general judgment will not be except on the day of resurrection, when the spirit comes and unites with the body, and man will be one [person], and he will be judged in spirit and body, as the Apostle said, "For we must all appear before the judgment seat of Christ, that each one may receive the things done in the body, according to what he has done, whether good or

---
820 Philippians 4:13.
821 Literally: old soul.

bad."[822]

As long as the matter is thus, we ask, "What does the author mean by 'the new man'?"

3. What is "the new man"? Is it a spirit only?

The author says:

> The meaning of this is perfectly clear, that the man who has received the Holy Spirit in Baptism, has drunk the divine Blood, has been nourished by the holy Body, has become a new man by these, receiving the Spirit of life in Christ, has accepted the Scriptures, and the commandments of Christ have become the law of his mind ... and he has been occupied with them, and his will has become armed with them through the love of Christ and His goodness—then the mistakes and sins of the body will not prevail—but even the law of sin in its entirety that is working in the members—that man may be taken out from under the acceptance of God's justice and mercy. This means that there is no longer a condemnation against him, nor will there be. Why? Because, as we have previously proven, the commandments of Christ and His teachings are for the new man, that he may live.

Then he says:

> The weaknesses of the body will not be accounted against him, and this is according to God's justice and mercy. For man does not inherit eternal life through the works of the body, nor through the body in its entirety, but through the new man who has been disciplined by the Scriptures, whose will has rejoiced in the works of the Spirit, and his intent has become sanctified from within by the holiness of Christ.

---

822   2 Corinthians 5:10.

Here there is a clear contradiction: How are there present mistakes, sins, and weaknesses of the body in a man whose will has rejoiced in the works of the Spirit, and his intent has become sanctified from within by the holiness of Christ, and his will has become armed through the love of Christ and His goodness?

And here the author attacks the body and says concerning it that it is merely a shell for the spirit.

4. Is the body merely a shell for the spirit?

The author says that the body is "merely the external shell or the transient vessel," in which the new man works. And after the new man completes his works ... and is made ready for the kingdom of heaven, "he throws away the body and sets off unobstructed to inhabit the heaven." And he says, "The body benefits nothing. For it offers absolutely nothing to the new man. Rather on the contrary, it hinders the growth of the new man in the spirit, and always pulls him to the earth with its desires and lusts. Therefore, it has become a vile burden upon the new man!"

Then he says:

> The place of the body with respect to the new man is the place of the contrary partner. For his continual running towards desires and lusts reveals the extent of the growth of the spiritual man and the hardness of his will ... "you do not do the things that you wish" (Galatians 5:17). Here the reader must be very attentive, [understanding] that man does in the body what the spirit does not want, as though the spirit is forced to it. This is a shameful image in which the body gains the upper hand with its lust, so it overcomes the new man and his spirit.

He also says, "Therefore, is it possible, because of the earthly disobedience of the body and its rebellion, that the new man would lose his wish, hope, and eternal life which he was called to? God forbid."

Here we respond, by saying: How can the new man be, with the disobedience of the body and its rebellion? And how, with the disobedience of the body and its rebellion, does man not lose eternal life? While the Scripture says that the lust of the flesh and the lust of the eyes are against the love of God[823], but are [even] "enmity with God"[824], and that "neither fornicators ... nor adulterers ... will inherit the kingdom of God."[825]

He speaks about a person as though he were two persons: the spirit walks in its righteousness, and the body walks in its disobedience; and there is no condemnation against the person.

The opposite is true. For the man, if he were born anew of water and the Spirit, this does not apply to his spirit only, but his body is anointed with the oil of Holy Anointing (Myron) 36 times on all the openings of his body and joints. And so he is sanctified, [both] body and spirit. And the new man is not the spirit only, but the spirit and body together. And when he sins, he sins, body and spirit.

Someone might say, "What guilt does the spirit have in the sin of the body?" We say that because the spirit was subject to the body; therefore, the body prevailed over the spirit. And the spirit did not resist to the greatest degree which might bring back the body from its disobedience. If sin in its nature is a lack of love for God, then it is not the affair of the body only, but is a deviation of the spirit which made it surrender to the body in its sins.

5. Are we innocent and righteous, while in sin?

Sadly, the author says that this new man, "there is no longer a condemnation against him, and will not be," and, "The weaknesses of the body will not be accounted against him." But he says more than this: "Sin has gone out of the account of condemnation forever for the believers in His name. The basis of all this is that the bonds of sin per se were loosed from man finally and forever on the

---

823 See 1 John 2:15–16.
824 James 4:4.
825 1 Corinthians 6:9–10.

cross. For its price was paid fully." But even more than this, he says, "There is sin in us, yes, but there is no sin against us. Let us proceed to judgment [as] sinners, but we are justified. We are condemned to death, but the judgment was ripped up and lost the warrant for its execution, and death was cast out, and we received an everlasting exoneration[826] in Christ."

I absolutely , however, do not agree with the author on his expression "we received an everlasting exoneration." Exoneration means that we are innocent and have no sin. But we are sinners, yet we received a pardon or remission, and not exoneration [i.e. not a "not guilty" sentence].

What is painful is that he repeats the same expression exactly, saying concerning the devil that "he makes us stand before God as condemned, and we are innocent, as condemned to death, and we are righteous in Christ and alive in Him." How are we righteous in Christ, and we are living in sin? The phrases "we are righteous" and "we are innocent" remind us of the story of the Pharisee and tax collector, where the Pharisee who boasted of his righteousness did not go down justified like the tax collector who confessed his sin[827]. Then how does the phrase "we are sinners" agree with the phrase "we are innocent"?

Persistently, the author says, "On the cross sin died, death was abolished, and the condemnation was annulled," and sometimes he adds, "with respect to believers." Faith alone is not sufficient without repentance. And sadly, the author did not mention the word "repentance" in all that which he prior said about the justification of man.

6. Is confession sufficient to justify man?

He says, "If the believer committed a sin, it would be forgiven him by merely confessing it." In reality, there is no remission of sin with confession without repentance. And the Mystery of Confession in the holy Church is called the Mystery of Repentance.

---

826 I.e. "not guilty."
827 See Luke 18:14.

There are many examples in the Scriptures of people who confessed their sin, but did not receive remission, like Achan the son of Carmi in the days of Joshua the son of Nun. He confessed his sin in detail[828], but he perished, and they stoned him, and he was not forgiven. Pharaoh also, in the days of Moses and Aaron, confessed his sin and said, "I have sinned this time. The LORD is righteous, and my people and I are wicked."[829] But he did not repent, so the Lord did not forgive him. And even Judas Iscariot confessed and said, "I have sinned by betraying innocent blood."[830] And he returned the silver which had taken, but the sin of Judas was not forgiven, and he perished.

Concerning the importance of repentance, the Lord says, "Unless you repent you will all likewise perish."[831] Confession only then is not sufficient, while the body remains an adversary, sinful, and a contrary partner of the spirit.

7. Did the devil establish in us "the conscience of sin"?

The author says:

> We declare with all sadness and sorrow that the devil has succeeded in polluting the conscience of believers once again. For many of the teachers still believe and teach that the believer's sins have still the ability to condemn him and kill him; and that because of his sins, he cannot be accepted by God nor see the light of eternal life; and that his defeat before the sins of the flesh, even those working in him according to the law of sin, is capable of depriving him of the kingdom of God.
>
> And thus, the devil succeeded in bringing back the sin's deadly authority once again, and bringing back the condemnation of death against man, as though Christ was not crucified, His blood was not shed, He did not die and

---

828 See Joshua 7:20–21.
829 Exodus 9:27.
830 Matthew 27:4.
831 Luke 13:3 and 13:5.

rise from the dead, He did not teach, nor did He grant us eternal life.

And thus, the devil succeeded, according to the teaching that does not belong to redemption, in establishing in us the conscience of sin once again.

Sin is sin, with which God is not pleased. It must be a cause of man's internal remorse and the rebuke of his conscience, because it distances man from God, making him in need of reconciliation to Him, as the Apostle said, "be reconciled to God."[832] So do we, according to the author's opinion, sin and run away from the rebuke of the conscience, feeling that this is from the devil who pollutes man by the conscience of sin? In our daily prayers, we pray the fiftieth psalm, in which David convicts himself before God, saying to Him, "Against You, You only, have I sinned, and done this evil in Your sight.... Purge me with hyssop, and I shall be clean; wash me, and I shall be whiter than snow."[833] So did the devil pollute David's soul with the conscience of sin? And are we polluted also with the conscience of sin when we pray this psalm and others like it?

If our consciences do not convict us, what do we say concerning the work of the Holy Spirit in us, who convicts us of sin[834]? Is this the work of the devil too? And is this of "the teaching that does not belong to redemption"?

8. Is sorrow for sin against the teaching of redemption?

The teaching of redemption is that Christ died on behalf of our sins on the cross. And it does not mean that He died on behalf of every sin of which man has not repented? For look, St. John the beloved says, "There is sin leading to death. I do not say that he should pray about that."[835] For the sin leading to death is that which is without repentance; it is the sin of those who die in their sins; therefore, we

---

832 2 Corinthians 5:27.
833 Psalms 51:4, 7.
834 See John 16:8.
835 1 John 5:16.

do not pray on their behalf.

But for man to remain in sin, without repenting, then we say concerning him, "as though Christ did not die nor grant us eternal life"—this is not a teaching according to the Scriptures.

9. Does the body pass away, and sin passes away with it?

The author says concerning that, "You sadden the heart of the One who endured the cross with its suffering, that you may rejoice. Therefore, we should be like, 'I am a sinner, but for the sake of the Crucified I am joyful, for my sin passes away with the body.'"

No, the body will not pass away, but will rise in the Day of Resurrection. Sin likewise does not pass away from the body, but passes away through repentance. As for sorrow because of sin, it is a duty, and tears also. And thus Paul the Apostle said to the Corinthians, that he made them sorrowful [which led] to repentance, and he rejoiced by that.[836]

---

836 2 Corinthians 7:8–10.

CHAPTER TWENTY-ONE

On the Incarnation

1. What is the teaching of St. Athanasius on the divine Incarnation?

St. Athanasius, who is the father of theology in all the catholic[837] Church, says concerning the goal of the divine Incarnation in his book *On the Incarnation of the Word*, that when man sinned and became subject to death and perdition according to the warning of the Lord to him in Genesis (2:17)[838], and when man was unable to save himself, therefore, Christ was incarnate and took a body capable of death, that through His death He may redeem man, in that He may die in his place[839].

Then the goal of the Incarnation is redemption and salvation. Therefore, we say in the Divine Liturgy, "Neither an angel nor an archangel, neither a patriarch nor a prophet, have You entrusted with our salvation, but You, without change, were incarnate and became man."[840]

This is likewise what we say concerning the Lord Christ in the Orthodox Creed, "Who for us men and for our salvation came down from heaven, was incarnate of the Holy Spirit and of the Virgin Mary, and became man. And He was crucified for us under

---

837   I.e. universal.
838   See Athanasius *On the Incarnation of the Word* 3 (NPNF² 4).
839   See Athanasius *On the Incarnation of the Word* 9 (NPNF² 4).
840   The Divine Liturgy According to St. Gregory – Prayer of Reconciliation.

Pontius Pilate."

But some [people] wrote on the doctrine of the Incarnation and complicated it with their interpretations.

2. Was the goal of the Incarnation love, and not the fulfillment of divine justice?

This is what the author says in his book on Paul the Apostle. We say that the love of God for man is clear from [the time of] his creation, [God] having created him in His image, according to His likeness, and blessed him, and gave him authority over all the creatures of the earth.

The Divine Liturgy according to St. Gregory is full of [words of] gratitude for all these, in which we say, "You have raised heaven as a roof for me, and established the earth for me to walk upon. For my sake, You have bound the sea. For my sake, You have manifested the nature of animals.... You have not left me in need of any of the works of Your honor."[841]

And God, in the Old Testament, says, "I have loved you with an everlasting love;"[842] "I have inscribed you on the palms of My hands."[843] And love was made manifest in the care and protection, and [in] sending the prophets, shepherds, and judges: "You have given me the Law as a help."[844]

As for the Incarnation, its fundamental goal was redemption and propitiation, as it was said in the Scripture, "But when the fullness of the time had come, God sent forth His Son, born of a woman, born under the law, to redeem those who were under the law."[845] Therefore, God sent His Son, "that whoever believes in Him should not perish but have everlasting life,"[846] and sent Him

---

841 The Divine Liturgy According to St. Gregory – Agios (Holy).
842 Jeremiah 31:3.
843 Isaiah 49:16.
844 The Divine Liturgy According to St. Gregory – Agios (Holy).
845 Galatians 4:4–5.
846 John 3:16.

"to be the propitiation for our sins."[847] Out of His love He did these, but the goal was our salvation.

3. Was adoption the purpose of the Incarnation?

No, for adoption was present in the Old Testament. For St. Paul the Apostle said concerning the Jews, "to whom pertain the adoption, the glory, the covenants, the giving of the law."[848] And God Himself said concerning them, "I have nourished and brought up children, and they have rebelled against Me,"[849] and Isaiah the prophet said, "But now, O LORD, You are our Father."[850]

Then the goal of the Incarnation is not adoption, for God from the beginning considered us sons, and it was said concerning Adam that he was "the son of God."[851]

4. Was the Church in the Incarnation born with Christ from the Virgin?

Thus he says in his book, that the Virgin gave birth to Christ united with her [i.e. the Church] with the Divinity, so Bethlehem "became the birthplace of the redeemed humanity."

The phrase "united with the Divinity" is of course not in agreement with the Scriptures, nor with any theologian. For the Lord Christ is the only one who is united with the Divinity from the holy conception. If the Church were the body of Christ, and Christ being the head, then the head only is united with the Divinity, and not the body.

As for the claim that the Church were born from the Virgin with Christ, this idea presents many complications concerning the question, "When was the Church born?" Was the Church born with Christ the day He was born? Or was she born on the Day of

---

847 1 John 4:10.
848 Romans 9:4.
849 Isaiah 1:2.
850 Isaiah 64:8.
851 Luke 3:38.

Pentecost? And the author has a book titled, "The Day of Pentecost and the Nativity of the Church."

Or was the Church, as the congregation of the believers, born first as individuals, then afterwards as a congregation? The Virgin "believed ... those things which were told her from the Lord."[852] Also Elizabeth believed, by saying, "Why is this granted to me, that the mother of my Lord should come to me?"[853] And of course, John the Baptist believed, who leaped in the womb for joy"[854] Likewise, Joseph the carpenter believed, when he heard the testimony of the angel.[855] And the circle of the believers grew bigger, to include the twelve[856] and then the seventy apostles, and others beside them. These were the nucleus of the first Church (the congregation of the believers) before the Church was formed as an establishment on the Day of Pentecost, when three thousand [souls] believed and were baptized. "And the Lord added to the church daily those who were being saved."[857]

Or is the birthday of the Church continual, through faith and Baptism? For everyday new members are joining the Church, who are born of water and the Spirit.

The phrase "The birth of the Church from the Virgin, united with the Divinity" no one has [ever] said and no one has accepted, except those who published a book, putting as a title of the book on the cover, *The Church: A Human Nature United with a Divine Nature*, in a manifest equality with Christ. And inside their book, they devoted a full chapter on "Bethlehem is the Birthplace of the Redeemed Church," repeating what came in their teacher's book, including many explanations.

5. Is the Church an extension of the divine Incarnation?

---

852   Luke 1:45.
853   Luke 1:43.
854   See Luke 1:44.
855   See Matthew 1:20–23.
856   See Matthew 10.
857   Acts 2:47.

This phrase is repeated in the author's book, and it was even made a title for the third chapter of this book, where he also says that the Church "becomes an extension of the indescribable, hypostatic oneness which Christ made between His Divinity and His humanity."

So have we, as a Church, as a congregation of the believers, become an extension of the hypostatic oneness in Christ between His Divinity and His humanity? What is then the difference between us and the Lord Christ? Is it equality? Or is it that which the author expressed in one of his books when he spoke about Pentecost and the descent of the Holy Spirit upon the disciples in the upper room? And he said:

> [The Spirit] descended as tongues as though of fire and sat upon each of them. Then we are [standing] before a "bush burning with fire," according to the symbol; or a Divine nature united with a human nature, according to the explanation of the symbol; or the image of the prophecy of the Nativity of Christ, as we have received [it] from Holy Tradition!

It is as though what happened on Pentecost is exactly as that which happened in the birth of Christ. He repeats the same meaning, then says immediately after that:

> The descent of the Holy Spirit, then, on the Day of Pentecost does not point to the bestowal of a mere spiritual power, nor the bestowal of gifts and talents, randomly. Rather, the matter is very serious, for here there is a mystical sign that an invisible union took place between a Divine nature and a human nature.

It is known, according to our faith, that the only One in whom the Divine nature was united to the human nature is the Lord Christ—glory be to Him. Did the disciples, therefore, become on Pentecost perfectly like Christ? God, forgive.

And he does not say this concerning the disciples of Christ only, regarding the change that affected their nature, but adds, saying, "It is important that we note that the change or renewal was not individual but collective," that is, "it happened in the nature of the first Church." And he concludes this by saying, "Christ united with the Church, so the Church acquired all that belongs to Christ... That which began in Bethlehem happened and was completed in the upper room." That is, the story of the glorious Nativity recurs on Pentecost, and the Church became a human nature united with a Divine nature, and the Church acquired all that belongs to Christ!

He also says, "The purpose of the Divine Incarnation reached its pinnacle on the Day of Pentecost, when all became in Christ." Or perhaps he means when all became as Christ! And here we ask a dangerous question: Did the Church acquire all that belongs to Christ?

6. Did the Church acquire all that belongs to Christ?

How dangerous is the phrase "all that belongs to Christ."

Christ has divine attributes. It is impossible for the Church to acquire these. Christ is from everlasting; Christ is holy, alone without sin, and perfect in His holiness. So did the Church acquire His being from everlasting and His perfect holiness which is by nature? Christ has the power of creation, so did the Church acquire this too? Christ is omnipresent, is omnipotent, who knows what is in the hearts and thoughts. So did the Church acquire all these, as in the phrase "all that belongs to Christ"? Christ will come in His glory to judge everyone according to their deeds, so did the Church acquire this? Christ also is infinite and has His absolute perfection, so did the Church acquire these two attributes also? So is the case with the rest of the attributes of Christ which belong only to Him alone.

Therefore, I have often said that the use of the word "all" in theological expressions easily makes an author fall into horrific errors, if it is used without care.

The author repeats the phrase "all that belongs to Christ,"

which he said in one of his books, in another book of his, saying, "Then the work of the Holy Spirit in our new man is to give us all that belongs to Christ, that we may be fit for the constant union in Him."

The author, in his book, then says, "The Church is considered an extension of the immense Divine body which fills heaven and earth. And the mystery of the Church is considered an extension of the indescribable mystery of the Divine Incarnation, that is, the mystery of the union of the Divinity with the humanity in Christ."

This is a repetition of the same thought [or idea] and an insistence on it. So is there in the Church a union between the Divinity and humanity? Did we become gods? Or we became like Christ? Or we became a Christ? Or is this [the same as] what he repeated in another one of his books? Or is the matter a sharing in the Divine nature?

7. Does the Church share in the Divine nature?

The author says in his book:

> And so, the Church is shown to be fundamentally standing upon sharing the Divine nature through the Holy Spirit. And by that she is shown in the depth of her being, that she is a unity between the Divinity and humanity through the Holy Spirit, as an extension of the hypostatic unity which was accomplished in Christ.

That is, there is a kind of equality between Christ and people, the members of the Church, in the unity between the Divinity and the humanity.

And he says in another book of his, "The descent of the Holy Spirit and the partaking in the Divine nature;" and, "Man became a partner in the Divine nature in that he restored the image of God and His likeness."

This is a clear error in understanding the meaning of the creation of man in the image of God and according to His likeness.

For God did not at all create man [as] His partner in the Divine nature. Otherwise, it would have been impossible for man to fall.

The author concludes an article in his book, by saying, "The birth of Christ is a mystical birth of the essence of the Church, to the extent that the body of Christ is the mystical truth of the Church."

8. Does the Incarnation have no limits, and includes the entire humankind?

The author advances to say that the Divine Incarnation does not include the Church alone, but includes all men. The author says in his book, "Christ was born in the body, of the Spirit of God and of the Virgin. It is a Divine body, holy, expansive, has no limits, includes the entire humankind through adoption."

And he says, "Sonship to God has become widespread over the whole earth, to all the sons of men, in the Nativity of Christ." And he says on the same page that "it is a gift of God through the Nativity of Christ, [He] having lifted humanity in Him to the degree of His sonship. So all were called sons of God! And sons are equal in everything."

The phrase "[He] having lifted humanity in Him to the degree of His sonship" is absolutely unacceptable theologically. For the sonship of Christ by the Father is a natural sonship, of His essence and His Divinity. It is impossible for any human being to be raised to it. Therefore, He was called the Only begotten[858]. So how is it then said that He lifted humanity in Him to the degree of His sonship?

We are sons through adoption, or we are children through faith. "But as many as received Him, to them He gave the right to become children of God, to those who believe in His name."[859] So how is it said then concerning unbelievers that they are children of God?

---

858   John 3:16, 18; 1 John 4:9; John 1:18.
859   John 1:12.

We are likewise children of God through love, as St. John the Apostle says, "Behold what manner of love the Father has bestowed on us, that we should be called children of God!"[860]

Virtue became a sign indicating the children of God, as the Apostle said also, "If you know that He is righteous, you know that everyone who practices righteousness is born of Him."[861] And he also said, "In this the children of God and the children of the devil are manifest."[862] Therefore, "whoever is born of God does not sin."[863] But the Lord Christ said that the leaders of the Jews who were sinners in His days, were not even worthy of the title "sons of Abraham," so He rebuked them, saying, "If you were Abraham's children, you would do the works of Abraham.... You are of your father the devil, and the desires of your father you want to do."[864] So how is it said that all men are sons of God?

The author advances in his words more than that, so he says in his book:

> Christianity is not worthy of its name unless it opens up, in spirit, onto the new humanity which sees in God a Father of all men, and Christ a body of every human being without distinction, where the doctrinal barriers are lifted, which were fashioned by the hand of enmity, of conceit, of partisanship, of blind fanaticism.

We stand in amazement before the phrase "the doctrinal barriers are lifted." Are they lifted between a religion and another, between an ideology and another, and all are made into one, despite the difference in faith and doctrine? And were these doctrinal barriers fashioned by the hand of enmity—and not by the hand defending the faith? What does he say then about the Ecumenical Councils? Were they also fashioned by the hand of blind fanaticism, according to his saying? How then are the doctrinal barriers lifted? Is that

---

860   1 John 3:1.
861   1 John 2:29.
862   1 John 3:10.
863   1 John 5:18; see also 1 John 3:10.
864   John 8:39, 44.

matter this easy, in the manner of which he speaks? "And the march of renewal begins and the building of the large body of humanity," according to his expression.

The author, also, in his book about the Incarnation of the Lord Christ, uses repeatedly the phrase "the body of our humanity," and he says, for example, "He died through us, and we died with Him," and, "He was crucified through us, died through us, arose through us."

9. Did Christ die through us, and arose and ascended through us?

We will give an example of what he said in his interpretation of the epistle to the Galatians only. He says:

> He who died through us, and we died with Him, is a Son. For the temporal event became eternal, absolute.... For we are dead and risen in Christ.... We have completed our death through His death... and completed our resurrection through His resurrection... for it is a power which lifted us above the earth and time.

He also says:

> For we died with Christ and arose with Him. For He died through us and arose through us. Through the power of death we descended into Hades[865] and completed the maximum punishment and judgment which was imposed on us as sinners and transgressors. And by the power of the resurrection we ascended and rose up from Hades and the pit—but from the earth itself—to[866] God, that we may live with Him in Christ.

Does anyone believe that we descended into Hades and the pit, that we completed the maximum punishment and judgment which was imposed on us, and then we ascended to heaven, to God? If we

---
865 Literally: the pit.
866 Arabic text adds here: the domain of.

had done all these, what has Christ done for our sakes? And did we ourselves complete the punishment, or is Christ the One who suffered for our sakes?

And those who were in Hades, who had died on the hope—did these complete their punishment and ascended to heaven, or was Christ the One who "descended into the lower parts of the earth"[867] and "led captivity captive, and gave gifts to men"[868]? Was He not the One who opened the door of Paradise and let all these go in?

Why does the author here disregard the work of Christ, as though men themselves are the ones who accomplished the work? The writer continues to say:

> And the sentence which we have fulfilled through our death with Christ is extensive, extending to all sins, and so much more the deadly act of sin. And so we have become innocent for good of sin as a deadly act. So, sin no longer has authority; neither does the one, who has authority to make [people] fall into sin, have authority over us.

So have these reached the measure of infallibility, they no longer sin, nor does sin have authority over them? Then the author says:

> For the power of our death.... With it we have overcome all the power of evil in the world. For the power of the death of Christ, in which we have shared, released us of every sin and every blame.... Therefore, it made us more than victorious. For it took us once and for all out of the sphere of conflict with the enemy.

Why then do we say every day, "Forgive us our sins"? Here the writer says, "Yes, the body may be harmed, but the spirit and soul are not touched. For we, with the body and in the body, may be found defeated, because the body is fallen under the powers of the world and time. But in the spirit, we are more than victorious."

There seems to be a contradiction here between "we are found

---

867 Ephesians 4:9.
868 Ephesians 4:8.

defeated" and "more than victorious." The phrase "more than victorious" reminds us also of the thought of Edward Isaac (the former monk Daniel of the monastery of Baramous) in his book *The Snare is Broken*, published in 1988, and in his book *How Great is His Beauty*, published 1986—the same expression with the same words.

Finally, my brethren, humble yourselves and do not think that sin no longer has authority over you, or that you have become more than victorious, for the true victory is at the end of man's life[869]. And always remember the saying of the Scripture, "Pride goes before destruction, and a haughty spirit before a fall."[870]

---

869 See Hebrews 13:7.
870 Proverbs 16:18.

CHAPTER TWENTY-TWO

On the Equality with the Lord Christ and with the Father

Introduction

The following dangerous questions, which we will address, emerge from the author's books and constitute theological concepts of the utmost danger, of which we fear for our children. And although they may not carry the phrase "the deification of man," they carry the same meaning, with details equating men with Christ, or equating the Church—which is the congregation of the believers—with Christ, and with the Father too.

From here stems the danger. For if men were equal with Christ, what distinction does He have apart from them in His Divinity? As for the equality with the Father, he ventures to [speak about] it in a manner the believers are not accustomed to at all. We will address these points one by one.

1. Are we a human nature united with a Divine nature?

The Lord Christ, in His Incarnation, is a Divine nature united with a human nature. So if the believers became like Him, concerning the union of the two natures, what would be the difference between men and Christ?

Nevertheless, the author has insisted on this since the

publication of his book in 1960. And he says that this happened to the disciples, representing the whole Church, when the Holy Spirit descended upon them in the upper room of Zion, on Pentecost, as tongues of fire, saying:

> Then we are [standing] before a "bush burning with fire," according to the symbol; or a Divine nature united with a human nature, according to the explanation of the symbol; or the image of the prophecy of the Nativity of Christ, as we have received [it] from Holy Tradition!

He did not deem it sufficient that this happened only to the Apostles, but mentioned that it included the whole Church, saying, "Christ united with the Church, so the Church acquired all that belongs to Christ… That which began in Bethlehem happened and was completed in the upper room." That which began in Bethlehem is the Divine Incarnation, the union of the Divine nature with the human nature in the Person of Christ. Nevertheless, the author of the book wants the matter to include the whole Church, and not just the Apostles representing her. Therefore, he said, "That which began in Bethlehem happened and was completed in the upper room."

He also said, "The purpose of the Divine Incarnation reached its pinnacle on the day of Pentecost."

He has repeated these words in all the printings of the book and also repeated them with the same terms, in another one of his books which was published in 1978 and was reprinted in 1988; that is, this thought has persisted with him throughout all these years, and, sadly, [it persists] until now. And he considers that "we have become partakers of the Divine nature and have united with God."

2. Were we born, as a Church, from the Virgin, united with the Divinity?

Concerning equality with the Lord Christ, he did not stop at the union of our human nature with the Divine nature only, but moved also to the birth from the Virgin. Indeed, this is what the author says in his book, where he says that the Church was born from the womb of the Virgin, united with the Divinity. "So it [Bethlehem] became the birthplace of the redeemed humanity."

The danger of this understanding is that it has passed to his disciples, so that they published a book, which they titled *The Church, the Bride of Christ: A Human Nature United with a Divine Nature*. That is, the entire congregation of the believers is considered to be a human nature united with a Divine nature, according to their understanding. And in this book, there is a long chapter which tries to confirm that Bethlehem is the birthplace of the redeemed humanity!

What is the influence of these words on our youth and children? Do they believe it and consider themselves as the Lord Christ completely, without any difference? And here they would be perplexed: If all are united with the Divine nature, how then do they sin? What does the union with the nature of God mean? "If we say that we have no sin, we deceive ourselves, and the truth is not in us."[871] Or do they receive consolation from another of the author's books, where he says that even if we sin in the body, we are more than victorious!

3. Does the Lord Christ dwell in us with the fullness of His Divinity?

This is what the author confirms in his book, saying, "It is true that the historical birthplace of Christ was a manger of mud, but spiritually, it is impossible that Christ dwells with the fullness of His Divinity except in man."

No, Christ dwells with the fullness of His Divinity everywhere, in heaven and on earth, and there is not a place where He is not present. But He does not dwell with the fullness of His Divinity in man, unless this were a hypostatic dwelling, and it becomes a heresy.

---

871 1 John 1:8.

The author repeats the same meaning, in a broader way. For he says in the same book concerning the resurrection of Christ in the flesh, "And after three days He arose through it [as] a spiritual temple whose salvation was accomplished that He may dwell in it. And we also live in it with the selfsame Divine fullness with the Father and the Son and the Holy Spirit. For where Christ dwells, [there] dwells the Divine fullness."

Who theologically dares say that he lives with the selfsame Divine fullness with the Holy Trinity? With the selfsame Divine fullness? Believe me that not even in heaven will we live with the selfsame Divine fullness with the Trinity. Our esteem will be raised, but we will be men and not gods.

As for the author's saying, "For where Christ dwells, [there] dwells the Divine fullness," this belongs to Him Himself as God. But His dwelling in man is not with the Divine fullness; rather, where Christ dwells, with respect to men, there dwells the blessing and grace and help, and not the Divine fullness.

Even the same verse, which the author used as the title for his book, says, "that Christ may dwell in your hearts through faith."[872] It says, "dwell through faith," and not "with the fullness of God." The phrase "the fullness of God" means what God permits of fullness for you—[that is,] the fullness God permits.

4. Does the fullness of the Divinity of the Father belong to us?

The author says in one of his books:

> The fullness of the Divinity dwelled in Christ bodily "and you are fully filled in Him"[873] (cf. Colossians 2:10). If we had the fullness of Christ pertaining to the Divinity, we would have the fullness of Christ pertaining to the Divinity immediately, and we would immediately have the fullness

---

872 Ephesians 3:17.
873 Translated from text. NKJV translation of this verse is as follows: "and you are complete in Him."

of the Divinity of the Father.

No, it is impossible that we would have the fullness of Christ pertaining to the Divinity, and it is impossible that we would have the fullness of the Divinity of the Father. If we had Christ's fullness of the Divinity and the Father's fullness of the Divinity, then we would have the power to create, and the power of holiness which is the Father's and Christ's. The phrase "and you are fully filled in Him" does not mean that we are full of His Divinity—absolutely not. Rather it means being full of His grace and His power which is working in us through His Divinity.

As for the phrase that we are full of all the Divinity of the Father and of all the Divinity of the Son, no one has ever dared to say this. Nevertheless, the author insists on it in the same book and on the same page.

The author says, "And in truth, the Father gave His fullness to Christ, that He may give it to us. And Christ Himself confessed this, 'And the glory which You gave Me I have given them, that they may be one just as We [the Father and the Son] are one' (John 17:22)."

Concerning the phrase "the Father gave His fullness to Christ," we say that all the fullness of the Divinity was Christ's not as a mere gift from the Father, but this was as a result of [the fact] that He and the Father are one nature and one essence.

As for the phrase "the Father gave His fullness to Christ, that He may give it to us," this means that the fullness of the Father and the fullness of the Son would belong to us! And this is not acceptable theologically, because it means that we become gods with all the fullness of the Divinity. Who said that His goal was to give us the fullness of the Divinity of Christ, knowing that He had this fullness from everlasting, before the Incarnation and before we existed?

As for the author's saying that Christ confessed this in saying "the glory which You gave Me I have given them," this is a use of the verse out of its place. The Lord Christ did not give His disciples the glory of the Divinity. Otherwise, fear would not have overtaken Peter in the same night, and he denied Him, cursed and swore, saying "I do not know the Man!"[874] And the rest of the disciples would not have feared, fled, and hid themselves in the upper room. How could this have happened, and they have taken the fullness of the Father? Christ did not give to His disciples the glory of the Divinity, for the Lord says in the Book of Isaiah concerning the glory of the Divinity, "My glory I will not give to another."[875]

Rather, the Lord Christ gave to them other glories befitting their humanity. He gave to them the glory of the archpriesthood, the pastoral glory which is His, the glory of the word and its influence, the gifts of the Holy Spirit, the glory of being witnesses, and gave to them that they may sit with Him in His kingdom. And it is impossible that He meant the glory of the Divinity.

5. Do we become filled with all the knowledge of Christ and all the knowledge of the Father?

This is what he says in one of his books, "If the Holy Spirit reached in us to the fullness of the knowledge of Christ, we become filled immediately with the fullness of the knowledge of the Father." How shocking!

God knows the hidden and manifest [things], knows what is in the hearts, thoughts, and intents. So do we ourselves reach to this fullness of knowledge? When the Apostles asked the Lord, before His ascension, concerning His Second Coming, He said to them, "It is not for you to know times or seasons which the Father has put in His own authority."[876] So will those who are filled with all the knowledge of the Father have more knowledge than the Apostles, and will know the things which the Father has put in His own authority?

And what about the knowledge of that day and hour, concerning which the Lord said that "no one knows, not even the

---

874 See Matthew 26:70–74.
875 Isaiah 42:8.
876 Acts 1:7.

angels in heaven"[877]? Will those, who will reach the fullness of the knowledge of the Father, know them, so that they know what the angels in heaven do not know?

This is a marvelous audacity, that someone would say, "we immediately become filled with the fullness of the knowledge of the Father." Our knowledge of the Father needs the whole eternal life, of which the Lord said, in His speech with the Father before going to Gethsemane, "This is eternal life, that they may know You, the only true God."[878] As for being filled with all the knowledge of the Father, no man will reach, a man who needs first to know himself.

6. Does the Holy Spirit give us all that belongs to Christ and all that belongs to the Father?

This is what the author says in one of his books, saying:

> The Holy Spirit is the Mediator between the Father and Christ, to make all that belongs to the Father the Son's in the Spirit. The Holy Spirit is the Mediator, standing between us and Christ, to give us all that belongs to Christ and all that belongs to the Father.

First of all, I would like to say that the Holy Spirit is the Spirit of the Father and at the same time He is the Spirit of the Son.

As for the phrase that the Holy Spirit gives us "all that belongs to Christ and all that belongs to the Father," theology does not accept it at all, for it is impossible for "all that belongs to Christ and all that belongs to the Father" to be contained in a book, nor can the whole universe contain also, nor can human nature bear. Many times I have said that using the word "all" in such theological matters has its dangers and leads to innumerable errors.

Of that belonging to the Father is His being from everlasting[879]. Were we given that we be from everlasting? He has

---

877 Mark 13:32.
878 John 17:3.
879 Arabic: *azalia*.

also omnipresence, omniscience, omnipotence, and the power of creation. Were we given all these? What about the judgment in the Second Coming? What about casting out evil men into outer darkness, and casting out Satan and the beast into the lake which burns with fire and brimstone? Were we given all these? He who has ears to hear, let him hear![880]

What about the fear of God and His majesty and His glory? When Christ appeared to John of the Revelation in some of this majesty, he could not bear it and said, "I fell at His feet as dead."[881] So how is it that we have all that belongs to the Father and all that belongs to Christ?

Believe me, these words require of a man to seek remission—even the mere thought that we would have all that belongs to the Father and all that belongs to Christ.

7. Did the Nativity of Christ lift humanity to the degree of His sonship?

The author says in one of his books, "It is a gift of God through the Nativity of Christ, [He] having lifted humanity in Him to the degree of His sonship. So, all were called sons of God! And sons are equal in everything."

Men became sons of God, but not all of humankind, for the Scripture says, "But as many as received Him, to them He gave the right to become children of God, to those who believe in His name."[882] Then not all of men [became sons of God], but only to those who received Him and believed [in Him].

What is dangerous in this statement is the saying "[He] having lifted humanity in Him to the degree of His sonship." The degree of the sonship of Christ no one has been lifted to it; therefore, He is called the only begotten Son[883]. For He is the only One who is of the essence of the Father, of His Divinity, and of His nature.

---

880 Matthew 13:40–43.
881 Revelation 1:17.
882 John 1:12.
883 John 3:16, 18; 1 John 4:9; John 1:18.

The phrase "[He] having lifted humanity in Him to the degree of His sonship" means equality with Christ! The believers have become sons, but not to the degree of the sonship of Christ. This is a theological error.

Finally, my sons, humble yourselves and do not [seek to] be deified, and do not claim that you have all that belongs to the Father and all that belongs to Christ, and do not say that you are a human nature united with a Divine nature. And always remember the saying of the Scripture, "Pride goes before destruction, and a haughty spirit before a fall."[884]

---

884 Proverbs 16:18.

www.ingramcontent.com/pod-product-compliance
Lightning Source LLC
Chambersburg PA
CBHW031625160426
43196CB00006B/284